"I recommend this very well-researched book to both trainee teachers and seasoned practitioners, like me, without hesitation. Its hands-on approach and implicit focus on the development of a professional identity make this a key 'go-to' reference source for serious educators."

Colin Wynne
Maricourt Catholic High School

"The expertise and experience that has been used to write this textbook is unrivalled and it will prove to become and essential resource for those training to become Business, Economics, and Enterprise teachers, as well as those who are currently in the profession. This textbook provides guidance and information that will not only help improve practice within the classroom, but also to engage with and encourage debate on some of the key issues which face the subject area over the coming years."

Daren Fairhurst
Head of Business and ICT, Pensby High School and Principal Fellow of the EBEA

TEACHING BUSINESS, ECONOMICS AND ENTERPRISE 14–19

This book provides core knowledge and guidance for successful teaching in Business, Economics, and Enterprise Education, and is based on the most up-to-date requirements. Written by experts with expertise in delivering business education in teacher training, further education, and secondary schools, it explores the nature of each subject in relation to the curriculum and offers subject-specific pedagogy to help develop teaching skills and confidence within the classroom.

Including case studies and reflective questions in every chapter, this book covers the key topics across the subjects such as:

* Financial literacy
* Planning for the delivery of academic and vocational subjects
* The value of different qualifications and business and industry links
* Strategies for successful differentiation
* Assessment and pupil progression

Teaching Business, Economics and Enterprise 14–19 is a vital resource for training or newly qualified teachers looking to deliver excellent teaching that will inspire their students and lead to successful learning.

Helena Knapton is the former PGCE Business Education Course Leader at Edge Hill University, UK. She is now Learning and Teaching Development Lead within the Faculty of Education at Edge Hill University, as well as a Senior Fellow of the Higher Education Academy.

Jamila Gurjee is a former Associate Tutor and Researcher, PGCE Business Education at Edge Hill University, UK. She has been teaching Business and Business-related subjects to students in secondary schools, sixth form, and for adult provision for the past 10 years. Having been Head of Department at a busy school in the South East, she is now teaching Law and Business at St.Mary's College in Blackburn.

Teaching Business, Economics and Enterprise 14–19

Helena Knapton and Jamila Gurjee

LONDON AND NEW YORK

First published 2020
by Routledge
2 Park Square, Milton Park, Abingdon, Oxon OX14 4RN

and by Routledge
52 Vanderbilt Avenue, New York, NY 10017

Routledge is an imprint of the Taylor & Francis Group, an informa business

British Library Cataloguing-in-Publication Data
A catalogue record for this book is available
from the British Library

Library of Congress Cataloging-in-Publication Data
A catalog record has been requested for this book

ISBN: 978-1-138-04550-7 (hardback)
ISBN: 978-1-138-04551-4 (paperback)
ISBN: 978-1-315-17194-4 (ebook)

Typeset in Bembo
by Cenveo® Publisher Services

FOR ALL OUR STUDENT TEACHERS

CONTENTS

PREFACE

Teaching Business, Economics and Enterprise Education has been written against a background of significant change in education and specifically within Initial Teacher Training (ITT) in England. While it is recognised that the intention of such changes is to improve the educational opportunities for young people, there have been unintended consequences as a result of frequent governmental interventions. For the Business and Economics teaching community this has been felt in the reduction of Higher Education Institution (HEI). *Business, Economics, and Enterprise Education* has been written against a background of significant change in education and specifically within Initial Teacher Training (ITT) in England. While it is recognised that the intention of such changes is to improve the educational opportunities for young people, there have been unintended consequences as a result of frequent governmental interventions. For the Business and Economics teaching community this has been felt in the reduction of Higher Education Institution (HEI)-led PGCE programmes and with school-led provision failing to fill the gap.

The title of the textbook reflects the identification of the subject area by Ofsted, i.e., Business, Economics, and Enterprise Education. It draws on the experience and expertise of the authors as school and Further Education (FE) teachers as well as deliverers of teacher training within Edge Hill University, and reflecting the current - and welcomed - emphasis on evidence-based teaching and learning.

A key purpose of this textbook is, therefore, to provide those who are Business or Economics subject specialists and who are new to the profession an introduction to key pedagogical themes and potential resources that will support their early development. It is also of use to those whose role is to support those new Business and Economics teachers, either in their role as PGCE Course Leaders or as school-based mentors. The reference lists are intended to provide the reader with the opportunity to review the texts used by the authors, with a chosen bias towards those sources that are available online for ease of access.

For the authors, being members of the Business, Economics, and Enterprise teaching community - this small part of the teaching profession - has been, and continues to be a rich and rewarding experience. We hope that this textbook supports readers in their development as practitioners and to enjoy for themselves the challenges and successes of this professional life.

1

INTRODUCTION

Introduction – starting teaching

Arriving at your first school can be exciting, daunting, nerve-racking, and intimidating. The thought of finally being in charge of your own group, and the progress of these groups, can provide you with a sense of direction, purpose, fulfillment, and perhaps nervousness. It is at this point that you feel you are beginning the real and actual element of your training – this is it! This is the beginning of your journey into teaching! This is the beginning of your leaving your footprint on the world!

Just as you have expectations of the support you will receive, or would like to receive from others, your school, your mentor, and the learners you have responsibility for will have expectations of you too. The school will expect you to maintain professional behaviour at all times. The school will expect you to follow the school's policies, procedures, and reporting system extremely closely. Your mentor will expect you to be organised, to be on time, to be proactive, and to be reactive. When you actually start to teach, your mentor will expect you to plan and prepare exciting and interesting lessons for your learners, which include all the elements of knowledge acquisition, assessment, time management, behaviour management and, ultimately progression. Your mentor will further expect you to follow all appropriate policies and reporting systems and to make well-thought-out decisions with regards to your workload and that of your learners. Perhaps the most overlooked or unexpected expectation is that of your learners. Surprisingly enough, they will expect you to deliver engaging and interesting lessons that will provide them with a sense of achievement and fulfillment, manage their behaviour, and provide them with evidence that they are progressing! In other words, these learners are going to be your biggest critics, and they will expect you to teach them, and teach them well so they don't feel like they have wasted an hour of their lives, which in their fast-paced world of social media and reality TV is precious and totally worth moaning about!

On arrival at your school, your Head of Department (HoD) or mentor will allocate you groups that will provide you with a wide range of teaching experiences. If you are on a teacher-training course, you should expect that these initial experiences will be carefully supervised. Hopefully, the course will begin with a period of observation to allow you to experience the structure of the day, the classroom routine, what is being taught and how learning strategies are being used, how behaviour is being managed, and how assessment is being used and monitored. As *actual* teaching happens, you can start generating your own ideas, creating a *bank* of strategies, techniques, and ideas that you know have worked well with learners and lead to good learning outcomes. Throughout your training, the observations you make and the questions you ask will allow your mentor to tailor his/her support and guidance to meet your needs. The mentor will be able to provide support, with advice and strategies that you need, as and when you need them, which you will probably take and carry with you for the rest of your teaching career.

At this stage of your career, the focus of your development will be on yourself, with a commitment to the learners you see in your classes. Each person has his/her own experience of what it means to become a teacher. Most commonly, new teachers will feel stretched and challenged, alternatively exhilarated and despairing – and always tired! Over time, as the business of teaching becomes embedded into daily practice, there comes a recognition that there are other significant stakeholders who need to be taken account of, i.e. colleagues, parents of learners, and the Office for Standards in Education, (Ofsted). If politicians are to be believed, the state of the economy is dependent upon the work of teachers too.

Not only do teachers have to deal with this range of stakeholders, but education is an area that is subject to government intervention - or interference - more than other parts of the economy. As such, teachers and lecturers are subject to managing the changes that successive governments introduce. It is impossible to navigate a course through these changes and deal with competing stakeholders without having a strong sense of iden-tity and agency. This is why the challenge of writing this book has been undertaken. In particular, this book has been written for those of you who are at the start of your profession, whether in the schools' sector or working within Further Education (FE) and Training. This includes those of you at the beginning a Postgraduate Certificate in Education (PGCE) course, are a Newly Qualified Teacher (NQT), in the second year of training within the FE sector, or a Recently Qualified Teacher (RQT). We have also been mindful of those of you who are at that point of your first transition as you take on your first leadership position.

We are aware that you bring your own previous life experiences with you into your role of teacher. The majority of new teachers who come into the school system are younger than 25 years, having recently achieved their first degree. Traditionally, those training to teach Business and who are teaching within the FE sector include many mature entrants, with a significant number who are career changers. You all have a significant role to play in education and in enabling your learners to meet their own challenges in life. Business is a rich and challenging environment that requires both skills and knowledge in order to achieve success. It is our job to inspire our learners with the opportunities that lie before them and to give them the skills and confidence to succeed in life. How we meet these challenges will vary according to educational context, individual philosophy and our own personality.

Teacher training and teacher's standards

The Economics, Business, and Enterprise curricula have been designed predominantly for the 14–19 age phase. Consequently, the curricula encompass a range of material that is delivered in schools, sixth form colleges, and in FE Colleges. Therefore, a person can train for the FE Sector (which includes sixth form colleges as well as traditional FE Colleges) or the school sector, with each sector having its own set of standards and its own period of training. Technically, someone who has become a teacher in either sector is able to teach in both. However, at the time of this writing it still seems that someone trained within the school sector has more flexibility in choosing where to teach.

In terms of training to teach for the school sector, one of the changes under the current government has been the proliferation of routes into teaching in schools. The vast majority of training routes include a blend of delivery between school and/or college and university. As there are no providers of an undergraduate route into becoming a Business or Economics teacher, there is the expectation that he/she will have an appropriate subject degree and will complete their training with a post-graduate teaching qualification, usually the Post Graduate Certificate of Education (PGCE). During training, the new Business or Economics teacher will be assessed against the Teachers' Standards (2013) and will be recommended for Qualified Teacher Status (QTS) at the end of the training. During the first year of teaching, the new entrant is described as a 'Newly Qualified Teacher' (NQT). This status of Qualified Teacher is reviewed at the end of a full year of teaching. Where the candidate is successful, he/she will then be designated as a Recently Qualified Teacher (RQT).

Within the FE sector deciding on what teaching qualification to pursue is recognised as being confusing. The "full teaching qualification" for the sector is considered to be the Level 5 Diploma in Education and Training. This qualification may be subsumed into a PGCE or Certificate of Education, if awarded by a University. To gain this qualification, new teachers are expected to undertake a two-year period of training. The status of Qualified Teacher Learning and Skills (QTLS) is awarded by Ascentis, which in turn is governed by the Education and Training Foundation (ETF). The standards that teachers are assessed against are the Professional Standards for Teachers and Trainers in Education and Training - England (2014).

With the introduction of Academy schools and Academy chains, the government removed the requirement for these state schools to employ teachers with an accredited teaching qualification. This reflected the position that existed then - and continues to exist - within the independent schools' sector, i.e. fee-paying schools. While this may appear financially attractive, it does mean you are entering an environment that can be very demanding and may have limited support. Moreover, the PGCE is still considered to be the "gold standard" of teaching and schools. Whether in the state sector or in the independent sector, an applicant is expected to have a teaching qualification. This can be seen in the person specifications that are made available when schools are recruiting staff. The PGCE is a qualification that is not only recognised within England. It has an enviable reputation internationally and there are a significant number of teachers with the PGCE who go on to teach at international schools worldwide.

It is not the purpose of this book to debate the merits of the individual routes into teaching or to provide guidance on how to apply for them. It is worth noting the following about different routes into teaching:

- Each route has its own expectations for the amount of teaching a trainee teacher is required to undertake at each stage of training.
- The degree and type of support that is provided both from within the school/college/placement and from the training provider varies.
- Some routes provide the trainee teacher with a wider range of experience.
- The number of transferable credits at the Master's degree level that can be achieved during the course varies.
- Some routes put the emphasis on training students for a career in teaching, while other routes serve as a stepping-stone to other careers, whether in education or elsewhere.

We recognise that for those of you coming into teaching you will have very different experiences according to the programme that you are on as well as the individual contexts of schools and departments. The aim is to provide an introduction into those significant factors which will affect the way in which you approach your teaching and will give you the tools to continue to develop the quality of your teaching as you move through your career. Key to this will be the development of reflective practice. In other words, to give you as new teachers a sense of identity and agency to become the sort of teacher you want to be and enable learners in school to have the education that they deserve.

A 14-19 curriculum?

There is little to show that the 14–19 phase is something *natural* to the English educational system. This lack of consistency is clear from the development of the two sets of teaching standards for the schools and FE sectors. It is further evidenced by the National Curriculum. This sets out a set of statutory subjects and subject content, which continue through Key Stages 3 and 4, such as Mathematics, Science, English, and Computer Science, and does not include Economics or Business. There was a period when the delivery of Enterprise Education was a statutory requirement at Key Stage 4, but it was removed in 2012. Even though young people are expected to remain in education or training until they are 18 years, there is no such National Curriculum for the post-16 sector. There is, however, a concept of a statutory entitlement that provides a young person with a wide range of choice.

In recent years, there has been a further hardening of the distinction between the 11–16 age phase and post-16 education as a result of the measures used to assess the school system, i.e. the introduction of Progress 8 and the English Baccalaureate, which are both linked to the 11–16 age phase (more about these later). With both Progress 8 and the English Baccalaureate (and their forerunners), there is a significant emphasis on academic achievement and the opportunities to experience a wider curriculum, including vocational education, are lost. In contrast, while student achievement in the post-16 sector is benchmarked by Ofsted against the national criteria, the subjects are not specified, thus allowing the colleges (FE and sixth form) the freedom to develop their own curricula which is appropriate for the learners and the local employer and Higher Education Institution (HEI) context. Traditionally, sixth form colleges will deliver a range of academic qualifications, predominantly A levels. The FE college will provide a wide range of professional and vocational qualifications, which can range from Level 1 and extend up to undergraduate level.

Despite the fact that there has been a strong historical and structural pull towards two phases of 11–16 education and a post-16 education, there have been periodic movements towards the concept of a 14–19 education. It could be argued that this began in the late-1980s with the Technical and Vocational Education Initiative sponsored by the Employment Department, which existed in government at the time. While this had little impact on education policy, it did show that agencies outside of education wanted to influence what was being delivered within schools. This has been further manifested by the range of reports and reviews since the late-1980s that have been commissioned by employers, politicians, and higher education, which highlight the gaps in skills and knowledge of our young people when compared to their counterparts elsewhere in the world. The driver for this frequent commissioning and writing of reports is the fear that these gaps will result in a weaker English economy in the future as we will be unable to compete on the world stage.

While the reports have not had a direct impact on the development of 14–19 education, it does not mean that government has been immune to the need to reform the system for this age group with initiatives used to respond to the changing political and economic environment. One response to the perceived weaknesses in the skills development of young people has been the introduction of the Studio Schools from 2010 and the University Technical College (UTC) from 2013, both of which are designed specifically for the 14–19 age group. Studio Schools have a strong emphasis on enterprise and links with specific businesses, e.g. the Studio School, Liverpool has strong links with the gaming industry and its curriculum reflects this. A University Technical College will be sponsored by a specific university and the curriculum will reflect the specific strengths of that university, usually related to Science, Technology, Engineering, and Mathematics (STEM). In both instances, the aim is to develop a different model of education that goes beyond the narrow experience of the curriculum in established schools. Developing such schools has been challenging, not least of which because they are often competing with the schools the learners are moving from. As is the case with all schools, some are very successful and others are struggling with a sense of identity and direction, which has an impact on teaching.

An opportunity to revisit the 14–19 curriculum has been missed in the development of schools for the 14–19 age phase and the introduction of the statutory requirement for young people to be in education or training until the age of 18 years. That is not to say the curriculum has been ignored, as can be seen with the increased academic expectations for learners in 11–16 education.

Economics, Business, and Enterprise Education – its scope and variety

The background of an indistinct 14–19 curriculum plus other changes to the educational system has had an impact on all those delivering across this age phase, including those teaching the range of qualifications associated with Economics, Business, and

Enterprise. The choice of title for this text is one that reflects the Ofsted description for the subject area. This subject area is a rich curriculum covering a wide range of subjects, qualifications, delivery models, and taught in the broadest range of educational contexts possible. In terms of *subjects* taught, it includes not only Economics and Business, but also Accounting, Marketing, Human Resources, Travel and Tourism, Enterprise, and Entrepreneurship; the list goes on. Some of these will be recognised as being at the academic end of the spectrum, while others seem to be more vocational. However, all of the subjects mentioned can be studied at degree level. The Business and/or Economics educators need to be aware that they are not just preparing learners to complete the course with good grades. There is also an expectation that they will be preparing their learners for work or study *beyond* their qualifications. A way of preparing your learners for subsequent study or work is to ensure that your own subject knowledge is secure, i.e. it goes beyond the requirements of the specification (which describes the content and assessment objectives of the qualification). This is in terms of the nature and range of examples used within the classroom, which means keeping up to date with Business and Economic news. It also means you need to read beyond the texts that are promoted by the examination board. In recent years, there has been a trend to use degree-level questions to provide stretch and challenge for those students who are working at the top end of their Level 3 qualification, whether vocational or academic.

At the academic end of the qualifications available, A levels in Economics, Business, and to a lesser extent Law and Accounting may be taught. Of these qualifications, A level Business is the most popular and it is taught in a wide range of contexts, including schools, sixth form colleges, and FE Colleges. Some teachers may find they are delivering at a level higher than A level when they work within an FE College that delivers Higher National Diploma (HND) qualifications, which can be topped up to degree level by joining the third year of an appropriate degree. GCSE Business continues to be a popular choice in schools despite the challenges to the curriculum from the introduction of Progress 8 and the well-publicised funding difficulties within the sector.

There are a significant number of vocational business qualifications, the most popular of which are Business and Technology Education Council (BTEC) Business and the Cambridge Technical courses. These qualifications are available at Level 1 (below GCSE), Level 2 (equivalent to GCSE), and Level 3 (equivalent to A level). These are particularly popular courses within post-16 education in both the school and FE sectors. However, Level 1 BTEC Business is unlikely to be delivered within the school sector. With these qualifications, the assessment is predominantly coursework, which allows learners to develop a wider range of skills that may be considered to be more appropriate to employment. Having said that, Level 3 BTEC qualifications are widely recognised as a route into studying at a degree level. While transition to degree study following a BTEC qualification can require careful management, these learners are often extremely successful with the increased emphasis on university students developing employability skills while studying and the requirement to apply theoretical concepts to business practice.

Following the release of the *Review of Vocational Education - the Wolf Report* (2011), the range and nature of vocational qualifications came under significant scrutiny with questions of their equivalence to academic qualifications, the number of opportunities for coursework to be revised, the degree of rigour, and the way some schools were using them to meet government standards for learner achievement at the end of Key

Stage 4. Substantial changes have been made to vocational qualifications, particularly the BTEC suite of awards. Specifically, this has addressed issues around assessment, such as the introduction of examinations and limitations on the provision of feedback, as well as changes to the core modules to be studied in order to increase rigour and equity of provision.

After the release of the *Review of Vocational Education - the Wolf Report* (March 2011), the Department for Education developed a process of accreditation of all technical and vocational qualifications. The purpose was to identify those that are acceptable for use in the attainment data which schools are required to produce, and which can be found here: https://www.gov.uk/government/publications/2020-performance-tables-technical-and-vocational-qualifications.

Each school and college will determine the qualifications and subjects that are most appropriate for their learners according to the educational climate of the time. In recent years, there has been resurgence in the demand for Economics A level, which many consider to be at the most academic end of the qualifications. At the same time, many schools and colleges are offering either BTEC or Cambridge Technical qualifications as a way of improving the outcomes for both the student and educational setting. Between the traditional A levels and the vocational qualifications is the Applied General Level 3 Certificate in Applied Business and the Level 3 Extended Certificate in Applied Business, which combines aspects of the A level–style qualification with a significant contribution from coursework.

As for all teachers in schools, cross-curricular and extracurricular demands have increased in recent years where staff are required to deliver outside of their area of subject expertise. The Economics, Business, and Enterprise teacher may find that they play a key role in the delivery of Enterprise and/or Financial Literacy. Teachers may be involved in these initiatives either in terms of actual delivery, or by way of developing teaching materials and providing support to non-specialist teaching staff.

The breadth of the Economics, Business, and Enterprise curricula means it cannot have a single pedagogy that is the same for every subject area or that can transfer from school to school or from school to college. Rather, the teacher needs to be able to identify what pedagogy is appropriate according the student's need, the qualification that is being delivered, and the educational context. There will be those who would say that some qualifications require a particular delivery model, e.g. a more traditional and didactic model is most suitable for Economics A level. For a number of Business subjects, it could be argued that there is a need to incorporate experiential learning and problem-based learning as the main model for delivery. More recently, there has been the discussion that Enterprise Education itself is more about pedagogy than the delivery of content. As discussed in the Sykes Review (2010) the pedagogy for different subjects varies considerably and it cannot be a case of "one size fits all." Consequently, the material that is produced within this book must always be read with a keen awareness of your own context, your own practice, and to allow yourself to develop your own professionalism. Also, you are encouraged to take calculated risks to widen your practice for the benefit of your learners and to fuel your own enthusiasm for teaching.

Economics, Business, and Enterprise as a broad curriculum area continues to evolve to meet the needs of its stakeholders. Like all good businesses, change is necessary to keep stakeholders interested. As much as this curriculum area has introduced change by incorporating new topics to reflect today's business world and changing methods of assessment, some things remain the same; it still remains a subject area that welcomes learners of all abilities and aptitudes in its classrooms. At the GCSE level, this could be because the learners, inspired by programmes such as *The Apprentice* or *Dragons' Den*, quite fancy themselves as entrepreneurs and would like to know more about the subject. Or, quite sadly – and rather frankly – Business is in an option block with other subjects which learners have had experience of, and didn't enjoy at Key Stage 3, or, just didn't want to study at GCSE. At A Level, this could be because Business or Economics fit in with the suite of subjects they have chosen to fulfill their future aspirations. Regardless of the reason behind their choice of subject, the expectation remains that learners will progress and gain the necessary skills and knowledge needed to succeed in either achieving or exceeding their target grades.

Reflection point:

1 What were the factors that led to your own choice of study of Economics or Business?
2 What is your understanding of vocational qualifications? Where has that idea come from?
3 How do you think your subject should be taught? Why do you think that?
4 Are you prepared to change your mind?

Range of qualifications – who are they for?

The previous section introduced the breadth of the Business, Economics, and Enterprise curricula area and made mention of the different levels of qualifications available. This section seeks to describe the levels of qualifications further to see how these may suit the learners you meet in your teaching. The understanding is that those qualifications that are identified as being at a particular level are equivalent to each other in terms of difficulty and challenge for learners. A full list of qualifications at each level is available at:

https://www.gov.uk/what-different-qualification-levels-mean/list-of-qualification-levels.

Most new teachers are familiar with the idea of **Level 3 qualifications,** even if they do not have experience of the vocational and academic breadth available. Examples include: the Level 3 BTEC Business National Diploma, the Level 3 Cambridge Technical in Business Diploma, or A Levels, which are commonly delivered by Business and Economics teachers to learners who are post-16. The aim of these qualifications is to allow the learner to progress on to University or employment. Thus, the learner is expected to develop a range of knowledge, skills, and understanding at a detailed level.

Level 2 qualifications can also be either vocational or academic. GCSEs are the most common formal academic qualifications that learners will take at the age of 16. In most state schools, learners will take about 10 GCSEs with a clear focus on core subjects of Maths, English, and Science. However, in contrast to this, learners who may not have the skill set needed to succeed in GCSEs and wish to gain work-related skills can study an equivalent vocational qualification such as the Level 2 BTEC Business National Certificate or the Level 2 BTEC Business National Diploma. Each of the qualifications mentioned so far are commonly delivered within the school sector, although there is always the threat that the government will take them out of the accepted list of qualifications for inclusion in a school's return of learner achievement. Outside of the school sector, other Level 2 qualifications are available such as the Intermediate Apprenticeship and the Level 2 National Vocational Qualifications (NVQs). These courses provide learners with the opportunity to progress in their chosen career path, which may include further study. This may be through continuation to Level 3 vocational courses at a FE college, in a Sixth Form Centre, or A Level subjects.

Level 1 qualifications are less commonly encountered within schools but are more likely to be delivered within FE Colleges. These are foundation-level qualifications that introduce learners to vocational qualifications and provide them with the basic skills and knowledge they need for personal and work-related skills. For example, the BTEC Introductory Diploma in Business is a full-time Level 1 course that introduces learners to concepts such as: Rights and Responsibilities at Work, creating business documents, and recording business transactions.

These Level 1 courses are effective in providing learners who may not currently have the ability to succeed at the GCSE level a pathway through which they can gain the skills and knowledge necessary to help them progress onto a Level 2 course. In my opinion, the value in such courses can be in the sense of achievement that they provide to those low-ability learners who may be disengaged and may not even see the purpose of being in school. These vocational qualifications allow them to gain confidence in themselves and instil a can-do attitude, while allowing them to become familiar with basic course content, work-related skills, a qualification, and a real sense of achievement. The challenge for the teacher can be getting the pitch right. Teaching at such a basic level can be difficult.

Entry-level qualifications have no prerequisites of prior learning, and within them, have three levels of difficulty. As for those who study for Level 1 qualifications, these are suitable for those learners who may not be able to meet the demands and challenges of achieving a grade 5 at GCSE. The qualifications can be effective in boosting confidence in those learners who may, for example, have newly arrived in the country, and may not have the communication skills needed to express themselves adeptly. For them, as well as low-ability learners, such courses can be successful in providing learners with an introduction to the subject. In addition, the learners will acquire the skills of building a portfolio of work and, perhaps more importantly, gain a sense of achievement as they receive a certificate on completion of the course. These courses can be taught over a one- or two-year period alongside other GCSE subjects. The demands of teaching these courses should not be underestimated. Alongside a low aptitude for learning, learners could bring with them other issues - such as attendance and punctuality, behaviour, and commitment - which will need to be vigorously monitored and managed.

The majority of new teachers to the profession come expecting to teach at the more academic end of the qualification framework, i.e. Level 3. However, as the teachers gain experience at other levels then other ethical considerations will be challenged. The result of this may be that there is a conscious decision to teach on entry level and Level 1 qualifications in order to pursue a social justice agenda, particularly within the FE context. In Further Education, there will be those mature learners who "failed" at education when they were younger for a number of different reasons that did not have anything to do with their ability, e.g. undiagnosed dyslexia, low expectations of teachers, and external factors that had a profound impact on their ability to learn when they were teenagers. For such learners, the opportunity to re-engage with education can be transformative in the way they view themselves and the lives they go on to lead; the impact on the teacher is also transformative.

Reflection point:

1 What sort of learners do you want to teach – and why?
2 What are your own ethical tenets of education and how do they influence the decisions you make?

Recent changes in education

Government has huge power over education. Each successive Secretary of State for Education will argue that his/her policies are intended to drive up standards so that every child has the opportunity to pursue higher levels of academia and, therefore, access better employment prospects, with the resultant positive impact on the economy. The following sections provide an indicator of the recent changes to the educational landscape that will affect the Business and Economics teachers in the classroom.

Progress 8

The current version of measuring the quality of education within a school that enables learners to achieve academically is Progress 8. This uses a specified group of subjects at the GCSE (General Certificate in Secondary Education) level and – taking into account the learners' starting point to secondary school – will identify the group's level of progress by mapping this against national benchmarks. Maths and English are given particularly high status as they are seen as providing the gateway to better employment opportunities as well as academic progression. It also reflects concerns that as a nation we lag behind other countries in numeracy and literacy skills, and the fear that this will have a negative impact on the economy in the long term.

Alongside Maths and English (language and literature), Science subjects, Geography, History, Languages, and Computer Science are given significant status and are next in line to be considered within the Progress 8 measure. The argument for this is that these are subjects that are widely identified as facilitating entry into prestigious Universities and employment. By promoting the study of these subjects learners will not face barriers to social mobility by undertaking less-academic subjects.

Other academic or vocational subjects, including Business and Economics, are in the last set of subjects to be considered for Progress 8. On the one hand, this means that those subjects in this last group often find themselves competing against each other as a final option choice for learners entering Key Stage 4. This places pressure on departmental teaching staff to ensure they recruit the correct number of learners for the course and ensure they achieve success so that GCSE Business can remain a popular subject on the Key Stage 4 curriculum. Where teaching is lacklustre, it can mean that the school will minimise its exposure to Business and/or Economics, ultimately by removing the subjects from the curriculum. On the other hand, Business has always had to justify its inclusion in a school's curriculum at Key Stage 4 as a non-core subject and, as a consequence there are many departments that have already developed strategies to engage and enliven their delivery to the benefit of their learners. As one school leader put it: "We only need to be concerned with Progress 1, i.e., the progress of our learners in our subject."

Changes in qualifications

In addition, there are significant changes to the qualification system that learners undertake. Following the publication of the *Review of Vocational Education - The Wolf Report* (March 2011), the government has required qualifications to be robust and "fit for purpose" to meet the demands of employers for a more adept and well-informed employee as well as to prepare young people to be economically more productive in the future. As a result, examination boards under the direction of the Office for Qualifications and Examinations Regulation (Ofqual) made significant changes to their provision. Specifically, there has been a move to synoptic assessment (where the content of a whole qualification is assessed at one time), a move away from coursework and controlled assessment, and a rationalisation of the number and type of vocational qualifications that can be used by schools for their student achievement data.

GCSE grading

Furthermore, the way in which student achievement is recorded has also changed at the GCSE. There has been a graduated change from letters to numbers at the GCSE level, where 9 is the highest score a learner can achieve. This new grading system has caused much confusion to educators and learners alike, particularly given that not all GCSEs converted to numbers at the same time. No doubt, more confusion is yet to come when prospective employers try to grapple with this system when trying to shortlist our learners who hold these qualifications as prospective candidates for job interviews.

The disjointed nature of this becomes more apparent when you consider that not all subjects have changed at the same time. A levels have not received a similar grading facelift. While A Levels are in letters, GCSEs are now explained in numbers. To summarise these changes for Key Stage 4, a department is most likely to be measured through individual learner progress - regardless of their starting point, personal interest, or motivation - and achieve a suitable qualification in Business or Economics, which is a grade C, a standard Pass at 4, or a good pass at 5.

Separation of AS and A level qualifications

For all Business and Economics A level qualifications, there is no longer a requirement for a sitting exam at the AS level in order to achieve the full A level qualification. Rather, the A level is achieved through sitting exams at the end of a two-year programme of study. This has resulted in a significant decline in the number of entrants to AS level qualifications due to the costs to a school or college to enter students for the AS exam.

Conclusion

This chapter has identified who the book has been written for and the educational context into which you are entering. As is the case for the world of business and the economy, education is constantly changing, and this includes that of our subject area of

Business, Economics, and Enterprise. It is a privilege to be able to teach within such a rich and varied subject area and to be able to engage with learners of all academic abilities and backgrounds. This book will not give you the answers to every question you encounter, but it will give you food for thought and different ways of looking at some of the challenges that you face.

References

Department for Education. The Teachers' Standards (online). Available from: https://assets.publishing.service.gov.uk/government/uploads/system/uploads/attachment_data/file/665520/Teachers__Standards.pdf [Accessed 21 January 2019]

Department for Education. Approved qualifications (on-line). Available from: https://www.gov.uk/government/collections/school-performance-tables-about-the-data [Accessed 21 January 2019]

Department for Education. What qualification levels mean (online). Available from: https://www.gov.uk/what-different-qualification-levels-mean/list-of-qualification-levels [Accessed 21 January 2019]

Education and Training Foundation. Professional Standards for FE Teachers (online). Available from: http://www.et-foundation.co.uk/supporting/support-practitioners/professional-standards/ [Accessed 21 January 2019]

Wolf, Alison (2011). Review of Vocational Education - The Wolf Report. London: Department for Education (on-line). Available from: https://assets.publishing.service.gov.uk/government/uploads/system/uploads/attachment_data/file/180504/DFE-00031-2011.pdf [Accessed 21 January 2019]

Further reading

Education and Training Foundation FE Advice (online). Available from: https://www.feadvice.org.uk/ [Accessed 21 January 2019]

Education and Training Foundation Teaching qualifications for the FE & Skills sector (online). Available from: https://www.feadvice.org.uk/i-want-work-fe-skills-sector/i-want-be-teacher-fe-skills/teaching-qualifications-fe-skills-sector [Accessed 21 January 2019]

2

GETTING STARTED
Teaching academic subjects

- Introduction
- How do I begin?
- Academic subjects
- Developing a scheme of work
- The seating plan
- Planning and preparation
- Lesson objectives
- The starter
- The main body of the lesson
- Homework
- Revision/preparing for exams
- Visits and visitors
- Conclusion

Introduction

No matter which educational establishment you are allocated or personally select to carry out your teaching placement, there is an absolute certainty that you will be required to evidence that you are able to, initially, teach part of a lesson of an academic subject and then move on to teach a whole lesson, and graduate as a teacher with the skills to teach a series of lessons that allow learners to progress on the course, be that at GCSE or A Level. GCSE and A Level Economics or Business, or Business-related subjects are very popular amongst learners for the wide range of interesting topics that make up this dynamic subject area. On most academic Business courses there is a balance of topics that require explanation, analysis, and evaluation through which learners can provide specific business advice to the business, based on concepts and strategies that will allow the business to succeed against its competitors, and others that require numerical calculations that provide the basis for financial advice. With Economics courses, students are also required to analyse and evaluate the local, national, and international environment and be able to both explain and respond to individual aspects of these contexts.

A recent incident that involved my computer getting hacked brought to mind the mistake that we as educators make when it comes to teaching academic or exam-based subjects. We can assume that as soon as our learners are armed with the knowledge that they need to be able to analyse a business situation they will be able to provide a perfect response straight away. In reality, as in real life, we may not have grasped what the new information actually means, so we draw incorrect conclusions, get distracted by the wording, focus on all the wrong things, and not provide the response that (a) is correct, or (b) we have been taught by experts who know best. Learning from our life experiences, we need to ensure that we provide learners with plenty of opportunities through which they can master their skills and knowledge that will allow them to provide the correct response when it matters – when they have to think on their own in key assessments, which is how they can demonstrate the knowledge and learning they have mastered over the duration of the course. Learners should be allowed to make mistakes, allowed to correct them either independently based on teacher feedback, or – for those learners who need it – supported so that they learn how to correct their mistakes independently in order to be able to gain the level of qualification they desire.

In his book *An Ethic of Excellence*, Ron Berger (2003) reinforces the importance of providing learners with plenty of opportunities through which they can make errors and gradual improvements so that they can "hone and refine" their work. Through making the mistakes, identifying what the mistakes are, discussing methods of correction, and actually correcting the mistakes, learners are able to gain a higher level of learning through which they can become confident in troubleshooting and providing the correct response to an exam question. Not only is this beneficial for their academic achievement, but it can prove to be a motivating factor through which they can strive higher and attempt more challenging tasks in both their academic AND in their personal lives. Although, their final grade will depend on the competency through which they provide responses to scenario in hand, schools are not exam factories and learners are not there purely with the purpose of learning how to answer exam responses. Learners are there to gain knowledge, enhance it, enjoy the learning experience (including their time in the classroom), and acquire skills that they can carry with them for the rest of their lives. A whole host of questions may pop up in your mind in relation to this: *How do I teach key knowledge as well as provide learners with an enjoyable learning experience and exam skills at the same time? How do I maintain pace as well as find the time to review previous work often? How much work do I review? What is the process that I need to follow? What do I review and when? How do I get buy in from learners to ensure that they review their work often?*

From your own experience of being at school and University you may be able to remember the amount of time spent revising notes in preparation for class tests and exams. This reminding you that regular and consistent practice is important in striving to achieve the results through which our learners can achieve success. Athletes do this; they practice and practice and practice one skill to reach their best performance level. Our learners not only need to review newly acquired knowledge to become familiar with it, but they also need to practice being able to apply it effectively to different contexts to achieve their desired grades in the exam.

The aim of this chapter is to provide you with guidance through which you are better organised and prepared to teach the variety of classes that you may be allocated by your mentor, including integrating assessment opportunities through which learners can make sufficient progress. As the table at the start of this chapter indicates, there are many different facets to teaching academic subjects. This chapter both draws on and exemplifies material that appears in other chapters dealing with strategies and extending your expertise.

How do I begin?

Teaching academic subjects begins even before you have placed a foot in the classroom. You need to become familiar with - and perhaps analyse - specifications, schemes of work, seating plans, lesson plans, learner data and information before you even deliver your very first whole-group activity.

The very first thing that you need to do is find out which course you will be teaching. You need to learn the full name of the course, the level and the unit you will be teaching. Find out the **course code,** so that when you are researching the course you can make sure that you look at the correct examination specifications and the correct course content. You will usually be provided with this information during your initial meeting with your mentor. This meeting can be quite overwhelming due to the sheer amount of information that needs to be passed on. Mentors generally want trainees to get "stuck in," as this is the best way to start in your placement. They will strive to provide you with as much information as possible so that you can "hit the ground running." It may seem like a huge "information dump," which you probably have to process gradually and in small chunks, over a few days or so.

In order to support you in collating this vast array of information and other vital information in a more logical manner Figure 2.1 is a guide. It is structured to focus your thinking towards the information you should seek to gain to allow you to make a smooth start to your teaching experience. Figure 2.1 is not exhaustive, and you can devise your own questions to suit your needs. This sheet, with all the information that is collated can be used as a cover sheet for your file, so you always have the information to hand. Regardless of how you choose to use this document, to have all your information in one place is useful as a reference guide.

Researching the course and its content is vital in being able to know what the requirements of the course are. To some, this may seem obvious, whereas to others, it may not even be a thought that has entered their minds. This is no surprise. Arriving to your first placement school can be quite overwhelming. Navigating your way around the building, getting to know the staff and digesting the various bits and pieces of information that you are fed, in a relatively short space of time, can leave you feeling quite overwhelmed. It can even be difficult to begin to think of what you should be asking to fully prepare yourself for your time in the classroom. Being in school can be quite daunting and you may even feel that the expectation is that you should already know about the course, which may cause you to feel further unprepared.

Whatever your personal doubts and niggles are, once your mentor has made you aware of the exam board and the course that the school teaches, the first thing to do is examine the specification. I say examine because it is extremely important that you get a grasp of all of the requirements and where the group is up to in relation to completing the full course. This allows you to make links with the individual topics and be ready for some of the questions that learners may ask you as they seek to clarify their knowledge. The additional benefit of this is that you, yourself, can test learners as you teach the course holistically to allow learners to gain a deeper understanding of the concepts

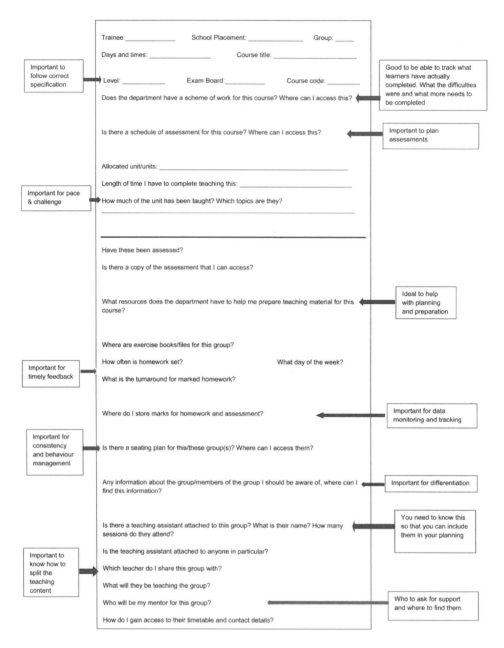

Figure 2.1 Example document to collate the necessary information to start preparing to teach a new subject and a new group.

and theories, as opposed to individual unconnected units, which leave their learning shallow and disjointed, further adding to your credibility as a teacher.

A good strategy to use is to check the resources that are available for each aspect of the specification. Look at chapters in the course textbook and see how the information is broken down, the activities that are suggested, and the assessment questions that are available. If you are feeling confident, you could look at past papers to gain an insight into how certain topics were assessed in previous years. Through this you will be able to understand the standard of learning that is required for learners to be sufficiently challenged, as well as prepare for formative and summative assessments.

Reflection point:

1 What were your motivations for going into teaching?
2 What Level 2 and Level 3 qualifications did you study? Were they academic, e.g. GCSE and A level or vocational, e.g. BTEC or Cambridge Technical?
3 Is teaching GCSE or A level subjects something that inspires or intimidates you?

Academic subjects

For many teachers, the motivation for pursuing a career in teaching is the opportunity to teach the academic qualifications within the subject areas of either Business and/or Economics. While this can be extremely rewarding to have the opportunity to work with learners who have the capability of achieving highly and with material that is stimulating, there are specific challenges that accompany this. It is an expectation that all who teach have a level of subject expertise that is higher than the level that they are delivering at. This means that teaching A level will require subject knowledge that is at degree level. This allows you to have a facility with the topics and you will be able to answer learners' questions with confidence, even when they are beyond the confines of the specification. It is one way that you develop your credibility with the learners, even if your understanding of the specification and assessment criteria is at an early stage of development.

Business and Economics are both significant subject areas at A level and at degree level. Given that the nature of degree programmes are that they are specialised in certain areas, the likelihood is that you will not have degree-level understanding of every topic you will be teaching. Where you lack confidence in your knowledge of a subject you will be expected to develop this confidence largely independently. An advantage of undertaking your teacher training at a University is that this gives you access to a huge array of resources that are written at degree level and that are available to you. I recommend that you make use of this access, even for those topics that you are not required to teach while on the teacher-training course.

Business and Economics (and Enterprise) are described as "live" subjects. This means that their content and the application of that content is in the "real world" that the learners inhabit. It is, therefore, your responsibility to ensure that those links between the content of their studies and the local, national, and international context can be made. In simple terms, this will mean having an understanding of the locality of the school and the businesses that exist in the neighbourhood, as well as keeping up to date with relevant national and international news. Your role will be to model this activity and adapt news stories for use in the classroom. Where your learners become participants in the search for relevant news stories there are a number of positive impacts. In some cases, this will be where you provide opportunities for "stretch and challenge," whether using real (but simplified) reports and accounts from public limited companies

17

for the interpretation of accounts or investigating the types of business in the town centre. This will be where you inspire your learners to have a genuine interest in the subject, rather than consumers of a qualification to take them to the next stage of their academic development. This can be through getting your learners to follow the likes of *Bloomberg* and economic journalists on Twitter or using *The Guardian* articles - either in hard copy or online - as a basis of your case studies.

Academic subjects generally mean that learners will complete either a GCSE or an A level qualification over the course of two years, at the end of which exams will be taken and a qualification obtained. There is no longer a coursework element. So learners need to be instilled with the correct skills and knowledge that will help them to achieve the grade that they aspire to achieve to fulfill their future goals and targets. I have alluded to this earlier on, and will reiterate this again, that the assumption is sometimes made that with academic subjects learners are provided and "taken through, or taught" the learning material, perhaps set a homework and an assessment on the topic, and then moved on by visiting the next topic. This is done in the belief that learners have the aptitude through which they can comfortably answer an exam question on that particular topic. Although this is how things seem on the surface, a lot more planning, preparation, learning, assessment, marking, creating, monitoring, nagging, revising, data capturing, and reporting takes place to get learners to the point that they want to be at for their personal success and satisfaction. The more familiar and fluent that learners are with the knowledge content and its application the better prepared they will be to achieve their desired grades.

Graham Nuthall (2007), in his book *The Hidden Lives of Learners*, advocates that learners should be allowed to revisit the same topic at least three times in as many weeks. Such multiple opportunities allow learners to gain a good grasp of the subject matter and can apply it to given scenarios. I gave this some thought and realised that this is what happens when we hear a new song on the radio. We listen to it once. When we hear it again, we recognise it, but don't know the words to it. By the time the song finishes, we may pick up the tune. When we hear the song again, we recognise the tune, and may pick up some of the words. The more frequently we hear the song, the better we become at singing along to the whole song and the more familiar we become with it. The more familiar we are with it, the easier we find it to add our own slant on it to make it unique to us. Similarly, if our learners have such frequent opportunities of learning, application, analysis, and evaluation then they are more likely to succeed in learning the correct knowledge and applying it to different exam questions to achieve their target grades. Therefore, it is important to remember to provide our learners with multiple learning opportunities of each topic. An easy rule to adopt is the 3 by 3 rule, where you expose learners to the learning material on three occasions in three different ways:

1 As a **define question** - To show basic, direct display of knowledge.
2 As part of a **multiple-choice quiz** - To provide reasoning of why it is a correct response.
3 As part of an **explanation** or a **compare-and-contrast question** - To examine the benefits and drawbacks and offer these as part of the explanation, thus requiring deeper knowledge.

You may feel that your time on placement is so short that the contribution to learner success is likely to be limited. In reality once learners have been exposed to learning that is fun, engaging, and challenging, they are less likely to forget it; this means that they will recall it more readily. This material is unlikely to be revisited, so it needs to be grasped by learners so that they can build on their knowledge and succeed on the course. In addition to this, the skills that you gain while on placement will be those that you will take forward to illustrate your skills as a teacher and provide evidence for the Teachers' Standards.

In order to meet these standards, you will have to demonstrate a variety of strategies through which you can show that you can guide learners through the teaching and learning which will allow them to achieve their qualification. Therefore, in order to help you grapple with all the different things you need to familiarise yourself with, I will take you through each of these strategies individually and explain why they are an important contribution to your lesson or teaching experience, whatever the case may be.

Developing a scheme of work

Alongside the information that you receive from your mentor, seek to find out what the learning needs of the group are. You may have been expecting to have groups that are "academically able" and self-motivated, particularly when teaching A level subjects. The reality is that the groups are always of mixed ability, and students will have different levels of motivation. In addition, you will have learners with specific learning needs. Therefore, in addition to finding out how many sessions a week you will teach the group, find out how the group prefers to learn; most of this data will be on the school system. There are many programmes that schools use to record learner information, so ask for access to these. They will help you plan lessons that are more likely to engage learners and provide them with a learning experience that is enjoyable and allow them to progress. Furthermore, finding out about the homework and assessment schedule (see Figure 2.1) will help you to plan and provide independent learning activities such as homework which you can use to reinforce learning, or as an assessment exercise which will allow you to monitor progress of learners. I always find it beneficial to ask for an example of a good lesson, and perhaps even find out what didn't go as well as the class teacher had hoped, so you know what the potential pitfalls could be.

With this information you can begin to draft your scheme of work. Figure 2.2 is an example of part of a scheme of work and you can see that it brings together the learning content and the length of time you have for the group of learners you have. Additionally, you can spend time thinking about how to link what is presently being taught with previously learnt material so that learners can remind themselves of what they have already learned and use that to learn to look at businesses holistically. Through this process of interleaving learners will have several opportunities to visit and re-visit individual topics. This allows learners to gain familiarity and confidence in the knowledge content as well as its application. To do this effectively include activities, starters, plenaries, homework and assessment and individual learning needs in your schemes of work. Awareness of learner needs is absolutely crucial enabling you to cater for your learners and make them feel that they are a valued member of the group that you are teaching. Not only is this important in providing them with the opportunities and resources they need to enjoy learning as part of this group, but through which they can achieve their potential.

Your scheme of work will further allow you to see the amount of content you have to deliver and how many hours you can dedicate to each topic. This is important in

Specification details	Length of time	Lesson objectives	Activities & resources	Learner needs	Links with previous learning
3.2.3 The role and importance of stakeholders The need to consider stakeholder needs when making decisions. Stakeholder needs and the possible overlap and conflict of these needs.	2.5 hours	Identify stakeholders of the given business. State what stakeholders will want and why. Suggest how businesses can keep all stakeholders happy when launching a new product or service. Identify the groups that have similar needs and those that have conflicting needs. Analyse the benefits and drawbacks for the business in meeting the needs of different stakeholders. Evaluate how they can satisfy each stakeholder group.	In **groups** – Give each group of learners a different business and the product/service that they offer – Ask them to identify and analyse the following: Who are stakeholders? What do they expect? What do they need? What would they be satisfied with? What does the business need to think about? How will the business keep all stakeholders happy? Will any of these decisions upset any of the stakeholders? How can the business remedy this? Which stakeholder needs conflict with the needs of other stakeholders? Why? How can the business help them through this? Why is this important for the business? Present to the rest of the group Once all groups have presented their ideas – look at similarities in findings of each group. **Resources** **Flip chart, marker pens, different businesses & products in envelopes. Camera, (to photograph responses and save in student area/print and stick in books)**	**H.A** Visual needs – seat at front. Large print. **A.S** Left handed – Do not seat next to right handed learner. **H.S** Short attention span easily distracted – seat at front.	Supply and demand Ethics Stakeholder mapping Financial decisions Growth

Objectives	Time	Activities	Assessment	Differentiation	Key words
Gain an understanding of influences on the relationship with stakeholders. Learn about how to manage the relationship with different stakeholders.	2 hours	Identify factors that will have a positive impact on stakeholder groups. How will the economic environment affect relationships with stakeholder groups? How will competitor action affect stakeholders? What is the impact of changing social trends on the relationship with stakeholders? Identify factors that will have a negative impact on stakeholder groups.	Groups of learners to be given selected businesses. Learners to identify stakeholders and place them in groups. (re-cap activity) Identify the factors that will affect the relationship between businesses and their stakeholder groups in a positive and negative way. How can the business manage the relationship so that it remains positive? If the relationship between the business and stakeholders weakens, how can the business improve it? Provide learners with scenarios of relationships with businesses working well/breaking down – learners to plan and write a report to advise the business of measures they can put in place to improve their relationships.	**Self, Peer & Teacher** **Homework:** Read the following scenario and suggest which stakeholder groups will be pleased with the proposal and which would not, give reasoning for your answer and advise the business on what they should do to meet the needs of all their stakeholders. Analyse the difficulties that the business may face with their proposal. **Scenario** **A global supermarket with huge buying power is planning on opening one of its stores in a quiet historic village which only has small family owned shops that have been there for hundreds of years. (18)**	H.A Visual needs – seat at front. Large print. A.S Left handed – Do not seat next to right handed learner. H.S Short attention span easily distracted – seat at front.	Ethics Stakeholder mapping Stakeholders Financial decisions Marketing Growth

Figure 2.2 Example of part of a scheme of work.

allowing you to gain an understanding of the pace at which you need to deliver each lesson and to ensure that all the content is delivered. The scheme of work acts almost as a timeline that broadly outlines what you will deliver and how you will deliver it so that the specification is completed ahead of the final exams. However, what you do need to remember is that the scheme of work is a working document, i.e. one that is flexible. So when adaptations need to be made, note these amendments on your scheme of work; don't rewrite the whole document. Other things that you could annotate on your scheme of work are things such as what learners found difficult to grasp and the additional time and strategies you had to adopt to allow learners to gain a suitable level of understanding of the topic. This will all help you to develop your practice as a teacher.

The seating plan

The role of the seating plan should not be underestimated. Figure 2.3 shows an example of a seating plan. The seating plan can singlehandedly change the whole ambience in the room. In my opinion, the first thing that the seating plan does is show the learner who is in charge. Taking away the power from learners to choose where they sit, and who they sit next to, can disarm them of their power to wreak havoc in your lesson. The seating plan could mean that you may need to change the classroom layout. Seek permission

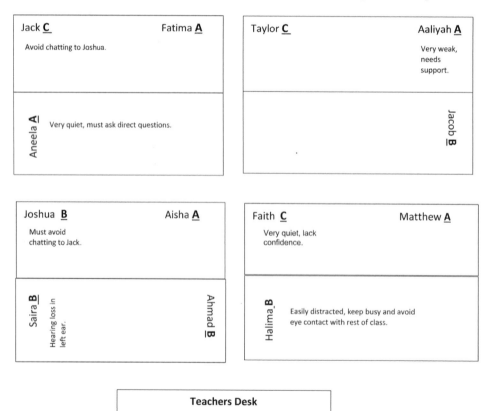

Figure 2.3 Example of a seating plan.

before you do this, especially if the room is shared with many teachers. The alternative is to put the furniture back to its original configuration after every lesson. The seating plan can either be met with enthusiasm from learners or outright resentment. Whatever the case, you have to deal with it. To prepare for any confrontation, try and run as many scenarios through your mind as possible, and preempt the response you may have to provide. For most learners, though, a change in the layout of the room can be a positive experience or a refreshing change, which allows them to feel more involved with other members of the group who they would probably never speak to or work with.

For the seating plan to be an effective behaviour management tool, research your learners by checking any data held about them on the school's monitoring systems as well as speaking to other members of the staff. This way you can make a well-informed decision about where best to seat learners so that they are more likely to engage with the learning material and less likely to try and chat with their friends. The fewer people that known troublemakers can make eye contact with the better. For progress, it is better to place learners in mixed ability groups. By having learners of a variety of abilities in each grouping, learners can help others out during grouped and paired activities. An effective way of using your seating plan is by drafting the layout with learner names, their target grades, and any other information you may have about them that may affect their learning.

One thing to remember is that seating plans are not set in stone; you can move learners around as often as you like. If you notice that something is not working in the first couple of lessons, switch learners around. And, if it does work, consider changing them around every half term to provide learners with the experience of working with a wide range of learners. The classroom is a safe place where social, as well as academic learning takes place and social skills are built and enhanced. Regularly changing the seating plan will inform learners of who their peers are, help them gain confidence in working and communicating with a wide range of individuals and build a learning network that they can lean on for support throughout the year.

Planning and preparation

Lesson plans are an essential tool that allow you to write down a detailed structure of your thought process behind the lesson. The lesson plan will allow you to demonstrate the approach you are going to take for learning to take place, the focus of the lesson, how you are going to deliver the lesson, the activities you will include, their timings, the resources you are going to need, and the groupings you will use. You can even make a note of the questions you will ask to find out learner views and opinions to make sure you ask the correct type and level of questions, carry out a baseline assessment, as well as ask probing questions to find out if learners have grasped the learning content.

If completed correctly, the lesson plan will allow both you and your mentor to visualise your lesson and address any potential issues. For example, if there are large blocks of teacher talk, then that may need addressing by building in mini activities to avoid learners drifting off and becoming disengaged. Similarly, if there are too many mini activities or one single activity that takes up a large chunk of the lesson, then that may need addressing because it may be difficult to assess the learning that is taking place and the level of progress being made. This is something else that you could discuss with your mentor and perhaps insert an assessment point. Your lesson plan will further allow you to plan for the differentiation needs; stretch and challenge, and assessment for learning strategies that will allow you to provide your learners with the best possible learning opportunities for engagement as well as success.

Your lesson plan is the place where you consider the rationale behind every single activity in the lesson. This is important as it provides a benchmark so that if the lesson does not work as envisaged then this can support your subsequent discussions and reflection with your mentor. This will then allow the discussion to focus on what you intended to achieve. Your mentor will be able to appreciate what you had in mind and be able to offer suggestions of how to improve the lesson, or aspects of the lesson, to gain what you had intended. In short, a well-structured lesson plan will allow you to identify the aspects of the lesson that worked well, as well as those that need improving, allowing you reflect and build a collection of strategies that you enjoy using and your learners will engage with. The following sections provide further detail regarding those significant elements that need to be accounted for in the lesson plan.

Lesson objectives

Lesson objectives are extremely important in setting out the theme and expectations of learning within a lesson and determining objectives should be the first part of preparing for a lesson. Both you and your learners must know *what* they are learning and *why* they are learning it. Therefore, after deciding what the learning objectives of the lesson are, they need to be shared with the learners at the start of the lesson. Providing an insight into what learners are going to be doing for the next hour or so can allow them to shut out what they have done in their previous lesson and prepare themselves for new learning with you. Consequently, objectives must be clear and effective in what you communicate to learners in terms of what your expectations of the learners for this particular lesson.

There are a variety of approaches that mentors, teachers, and schools promote within their context. In their book *Making Every Lesson Count: Six principles to support great teaching and learning,* Shaun Allison and Andy Tharby (2015) advocate that the commonly used approach of "All, Most, Some" structure of learning objectives conveys a message of low expectations of learners as it leaves them with the easy option of completing the "All and Most" activities, and then taking a back seat by deciding that they have done enough work, and that they are not part of the "Some," or, that they don't want to take the risk and get things wrong. See Figure 2.4. Alternatively, high achievers rush through the first objectives and only concentrate on the final objective. Shaun Allison and Andy Tharby (2015) advocate that a single challenging objective is far more aspirational as it guides all learners towards the same end point. This then leaves you, the teacher, with the power to decide how to support learners to achieve the objective.

Analyse and evaluate why businesses may find it difficult to keep all their stakeholders happy.

Instead of:	***All*** learners will be able to identify the various stakeholder groups of a business
	Most learners will be able to explain why businesses cannot keep all their stakeholders happy all of the time.
	Some learners will be able to analyse and evaluate the strategies that businesses may have to adopt to keep most their stakeholders happy most of the time.

Figure 2.4 Differentiated learning outcomes.

24

You could have a single objective:

The single objective not only allows all learners to feel that they are on an equal footing with each other but shows each and every one of your learners that the high expectations that you have of all of them are manageable and will allow them to strive to achieve that objective. This is because their thinking is channelled towards both the analysis and evaluation and not jarred by the "identifying of stakeholders." They will do that as they go along.

Although they may experience a "healthy struggle" (Shaun Allison and Andy Tharby, 2015:14), in reaching the end point, the activities and strategies that you use should be designed to allow all learners to achieve this objective to the best of their ability. One of the strategies that you could implement in aiming to achieve this is using mixed-ability style seating plans to allow higher-ability learners to discuss the activities with and support the lower-ability learners to achieve the learning objectives. To add rigour to this, whiteboard activities that allow each learner to take ownership and accountability of his/her own learning can further provide all learners with the opportunity of engaging in learning activities that are both challenging yet can be accomplished.

For example, whiteboard activities that first require learners to offer individual suggestions to questions are then discussed with the group. Learners discuss each other's responses to find out which one is the correct/best response to the question. The agreed-upon answer for the group can allow some opportunity to discuss the question together without learners feeling intimidated. Asking the weaker members of the group to present the suggested answer to the whole class can further place pressure on learners to take ownership of their learning, as they need to know "what they are talking about." This not only gives an insight into the role of objectives and their importance, but it also provides you with an insight of how the seating plan can support the teaching and learning activities of such challenging objectives.

The starter

The starter activity is important in focusing learners' minds on the learning that is about to take place, and the topic that will be the focus of the lesson. It is also a great assessment opportunity. In a short space of 10 minutes you can gain an understanding of what and how much learners can recall from the previous lesson(s). This interactive activity could also be used to engage learners by asking them to either work together to crack a code, or they can assess each other's answers to the mini test you have designed. A well-thought-out starter activity is not just a good way of settling learners, but it is one of the recap and review opportunities through which learners can reinforce and build on previous learning.

With this in mind, I set high expectations of all of my learners by making them aware that the first lesson of every week will involve a mini test of some sort, which will demand that they recall aspects of knowledge gained previously and apply it to a given scenario. This regular-spaced retrieval practice is recommended by Mark A. McDaniel and Peter C. Brown in their book *Make it Stick*. They assert that this form of quizzing of one or two initial define-and-explain questions, followed by an analysis or evaluation of part of a scenario "strengthens learning and connection to prior knowledge." This short and snappy activity, which takes about 10 to 12 minutes, is extremely valuable in revisiting old topics and keeping learners reminded of them. To make this a supportive task, learners are allowed an opportunity to discuss their answers with their peers first, and if they feel that they have given an incorrect answer then they can amend their answers with a different coloured pen before it is marked. This allows discussion and supported learning from peers, as opposed to a sense of failure and demotivation. Even the brightest of students will make mistakes at some time or another or will not have reviewed a particular set of notes.

This ongoing quick assessment imposes a sense of responsibility on learners to review their notes weekly. It allows them to gauge a sense of what they may not have grasped earlier and focus their revision and review on those particular topics. As they are afforded an opportunity to participate in dialogue with their peers, they have an additional dimension through which they are able to identify what they did wrong and why, through which they are able to hone their skills and knowledge on that particular topic. This simple starter activity, delivered in different ways, can provide multiple opportunities of reinforcement of their learning material because they are constantly reviewing their notes and not leaving *all* of their revision to the final couple of months before the exam.

For other lessons during the week, I use my judgement as to the type of starter that I use. If it is a lesson that they have first thing in the morning, then this will be a starter that will require some sort of interactive engagement involving discussion work or moving around the classroom. This is so that the learners "wake up." A popular activity for this type of starter is where some learners are given a question and other learners are given the answer. Each learner has to move around the room to find his/her partner.

If, however, the lesson is straight after break or lunchtime, then I will probably have a starter activity where the learners have to offer individual responses in a more calm and quiet manner to allow them to come down from the "high" of being able to roam free or run wild in the yard immediately before the lesson. This could be a code breaker or a multiple-choice activity. To get off to a smooth start, I ensure that all activity sheets are on the desks ready for learners as they arrive to class.

Reflection point: In lessons that you have observed:

1 Which starter activities do you consider to have been effective?
2 Can you identify the purposes of the different starter activities that you have seen?
3 What different approaches have you taken note of?

The main body of the lesson

When I mention the word *lessons* these are the words that come to mind: classroom, teaching and learning, assessment, support, progress and development, behaviour management, resources, questioning, data capture, and marking. The truth about the lesson is that for it to be effective in the classroom, it has to be planned and prepared prior to the time in the classroom. Figure 2.5 provides an example of a lesson plan that may be used at the start of training in order to ensure that all aspects of planning are taken into account. You will be expected to streamline and personalize the lesson plan to your own style as your experience develops and expertise is embedded in your practice.

There is a common misconception that all lessons should be made up of three distinct parts: the starter, the main activity, and the plenary. Although, this could be a broad outline, it is not a strict structure of what a lesson will always look like in its entirety.

Lesson plan					
Date, time & period	*Subject/topic*	*Curriculum links*	*Class/set*	*Room/lab*	*Total no. of students*
01.11.18 10:45 – 12:15	Stakeholders		12 Block A	B5	24

Prior learning/assessment to inform planning *(Please also refer to class list and seating plan)*

For example:
The role of stakeholders in the business, how individual stakeholder interest can guide business decisions.
Learners have very high target grades and are very able so the content will be quite challenging for all.
The seating plan is ideal for differentiated learning activities.
Peer learning for supportive, engaging active learning.
Support in the form of an individual scaffold sheet per activity is available for learners/groups of
  learners who may struggle.

Learning outcome

By the end of this lesson students will be able to……. *Analyse and evaluate why businesses may find it difficult to keep all of their stakeholders happy.*

Key vocabulary

stakeholders ethics standards	customers suppliers supply and demand	products services relationship	conflicts conflicting interests similar interests	reputation costs benefits

Cross curricular links, PHSEE, fundamental British values, Enterprise, innovative ideas & creative student opportunities

Enterprise, innovation, honesty, morality, following business rules and regulations

Learning & teaching plan

Time (mins)	Link to Learning Outcome number	Teacher Activity Objectives & Outcomes, Teaching Activities, Revisiting Outcomes & Consolidation	Learner Activity Identify the techniques used to differentiate for ALL Learners	Assessment Strategies Used to Ensure Progress of All Learners	Resources e.g. TEL, Other Adults, Materials and Equipment
0 – 20	**Starter and activity 1**	Assess previous learning – ask questions as per the PPT and provide allocated time.	Learners to look at questions on PPT and provide individual responses on white board – then confer with team and agree on single response. Allocated member to read out the response. Provide prompts and visual clues for weaker learners.	Check correct answer at correct level provided.	Whiteboards, marker pens & timer. Cue cards/ image sheet/ key words for weaker learners.

Figure 2.5 Example lesson plan.

20 – 35	**Activity 2**	Provide instructions for the advisory activity. Prompt learners to consider in full, the financial costs to a business in trying to keep all stakeholders happy?	Learners to use previous notes to advise the business of strategies to put in place to keep their stakeholders happy. Weak learners to be provided with possible response sheet that they could use to assist them in providing the correct advice. Learners to consider what the financial implications are and why they are important.	Teacher and peer assessment. Check: are learners calculating the losses and gains correctly? Have learners made correct connections between reputation and revenue?	Business scenarios and timer. Response sheet for weaker learners. Specific examples of financial losses/ financial gains to a business if a stakeholder was unhappy with the decisions that the business had made.
35 – 45	**Review point**	Quick **review** of which stakeholders a given business would have and how they would remain happy with a business. Explain the difficulties, conflicts and costs of keeping certain stakeholder groups happy.	Learners to respond to questions and suggest strategies that business could use to keep stakeholders happy. Learners to critique another groups response and as a higher advisory body provide additional suggestions.	Teacher and peer assessment.	Pens, markers, whiteboards & timer. Suggestions sheet of types of critique for weaker learners.
45 – 55	**Activity 3 (independent)**	Provide learners with the essay question, instruct learners that they have 10 minutes to read the question individually and make notes about the assessment question.	Read the question – think about the response, annotate the question and note ideas individually. Provide scaffold to those who are struggling	Check the level of response that learners are providing.	Question on PPT, and on paper for learners to annotate. Scaffolded exam question

Figure 2.5 (Continued)

55 – 65	**Activity 4 (group/ paired)**	Teacher to instruct learners to bring ideas together in teams to construct a plan of how to answer the question. For the teams or the individuals who may be struggling provide the support sheet. Discuss the areas of concern.	Learners to work together to write a plan for an answer to the essay question. Learners given different coloured pens to clearly show their contribution.	Check the correct information is being considered and that learners are channelling their thinking towards a correct structure to meet the assessment criteria.	A3 paper/flip chart different coloured pens for each learner.
65 – 70	**Review point**	Learners to be asked to re-cap why businesses find it hard to keep all individual stakeholder groups satisfied. What are the difficult decisions they may need to make in relation to keeping stakeholders satisfied?	Learners to be given examples for which one ultimate suggestion should be provided, of how the business can keep the stakeholder satisfied. Provide weaker learners with scenarios and possible outcomes, ask them to choose one justifying why they feel that is correct.	Teacher and peer Ensure correct vocabulary being demonstrated. Are learners making correct judgements? Are their any conflicts in learner thought process? Learners to suggest impact of conflict in logical manner.	Variety of scenarios. Scenarios and suggestions that weaker learners can put together.
70 – 85	**Write exam answer**	Learners to write the essay question under timed, exam conditions	All learners to work individually and under timed conditions to provide response to exam question using the plans they have produced.		Paper, spare pens & timer.

Figure 2.5 (Continued)

85 – 90	Learners to send snapchat to business that is struggling to keep a particular stakeholder group satisfied of what it can do to improve relations with them and what it may cost the business.	Snapchat question with business and stakeholder problem to respond to.

Home learning *(to enhance prior, existing or potential knowledge and skills)*

Learners to devise a poster using symbols and images only, illustrating the difficulties that businesses have in keeping stakeholders satisfied.
OR
Learners to write a report on a business that they are aware of, or have seen in the news which has either benefitted from stakeholder involvement or suffered a loss as the needs of an influential stakeholder have not been met.

Lesson evaluation

What was successful/not so successful? What was the impact of this on student progress?

Evaluation

Pupil Learning & Progression
Did all the pupils achieve the intended learning outcome? *(How do you know?*
How do you **and your pupils** know they have ALL made rapid progress?
Teaching & Classroom Management
How has your planning and teaching ensured positive behaviours, highly conducive to learning?
Planning & Subject Knowledge
How could you further develop pedagogy to address errors and misconceptions in your planning?
How could you develop imaginative and creative approaches to further match individual needs and interests?

Figure 2.5 (Continued)

As already indicated, the starter activity can be used in a number of ways. It is a great way to settle or invigorate learners, test their previous knowledge, or even to direct them towards the learning of the day. This portion of the lesson tends to be of short duration, from anything as little as 3 to 5 minutes or perhaps up to a maximum of 15 minutes.

Using the traditional view of a three-part lesson, this leaves the bulk of the lesson for the main activity, and 10 minutes at the end for a recap or plenary of what the purpose of the lesson was. A recent CPD session brought home the realisation of why this three-part lesson idea may not be effective for the purposes of teaching and learning. During this session, we actively participated in the teaching and learning, and after approximately 30 minutes the trainer asked us to explain what we had done in the first 10 minutes of the session. Much to our surprise and dismay, the majority of us struggled to efficiently recall how the session had started off. This showed us the importance of frequent review and recap of the learning material throughout the lesson.

Although not intended as a recommendation that you should stick to rigidly, I feel that mini review points could be planned at 20 to 30 minute intervals, especially where sessions are over an hour long. This is so that learners are given the opportunity to "pause and rewind," to reinforce and reconnect with the learning material, and to keep their thought process and learning on track. These mini "brain breaks" mean that the learners can process and reflect on the newly learnt information and start building their memory. This becomes a vital point in the lesson and allows learners an opportunity to gain confidence with the learning material, retaining more and using it as a building block to make links with previously learnt material, or perhaps make predictions of how what is being learnt now can relate to topics they may focus on in the future. Interim reviews can allow you to maintain pace, gauge how well learners are grasping the topic, and monitor progress. This enables you to identify how you can guide the lesson to better suit the needs of learners. For example, if during a review point you realise that learners haven't quite grasped what you needed them to learn, then you can revisit that information there and then, instead of allowing them to aimlessly try and complete work that they haven't fully grasped, leading to wasted learning time and opportunity.

As an example, a quick activity could be to ask learners to write down one or two key words from the lesson so far. This is then passed to someone at the opposite end of the classroom who will then write down his/her explanation of what the term that the first learner has provided. Another activity could be to ask learners to identify similarities and differences in key concepts, e.g. between gross profit margin and net profit margin in under one minute.

The classroom environment is a great place for learners to learn with their peers. As well as developing a range of strategies to support their own academic development, the classroom is the place where learners can participate in social learning in a safe way, which is important for their sense of belonging, personal development, and wellbeing. For this reason, as well as for reasons of progress and development, paired and group work activities are a good strategy to use through which learners can actively participate in learning activities and draw conclusions together. To avoid learners seeing paired and group activities as their time to have their own personal discussions, disengage with the learning material and take a back seat and become passive in their learning, using cooperative learning structures can help encourage active participation from all learners.

When working in small groups, the suggestion is that groups be of mixed ability. This is because if some members of the group struggle with a concept or activity, then another member of the group may be able to work out what the group needs to do. This not only ensures that all learners are able to complete the work set, but those who understand the underpinning academic concepts and activities are able to deepen their own understanding through having to express that understanding to other members of the group. To further encourage the involvement of all learners it helps to give each member an allocated role. This is so that every team member is engaged and has accountability for individual as well as whole-group responses. This may seem like a new concept for some and they may not like it initially, but I strongly believe that a sense of team spirit is created once they experience the success of working effectively in pairs or in groups.

Another way of way of developing the skills of working as a team is by using an approach that has been described as *jigsaw learning*. Each member of a group will be provided with a small chunk of information which is individual to them and makes up a part of the whole, i.e. a single piece of the jigsaw. By working together and putting the pieces of information provided together, they will be able to gain an understanding of the whole. To be effective, each learner has to break down the information individually to make sure that they understand it themselves. To further ensure that they have the correct understanding, they could discuss this with all the other learners from the other groups who have the same piece of information. They then go back to their original groups and take turns to teach each other the information they have and piece it together to have a comprehensive piece of material, which they can then use to answer a scenario-based question. To differentiate this, you could provide more able learners with the more complex/difficult aspects of the subject.

As an example, the topic of different types of business structures could be delivered using jigsaw learning. Working in groups of four, each member would be required to find out the definition, explanation, and an example of either a sole trader, a partnership, a private limited company, or a public limited company. As a form of quality control, all those in the class investigating sole traders would be expected to compare their notes and understanding in order to confirm the right understanding of the concept. The same approach would be used for each of the other types of business. It would be expected that you as the teacher would be part of the process of assessing the understanding of the individual concepts to make sure that everyone understands their own topic. Once there was common agreement, then each learner would return to his/her original group to share his/her understanding with the other members. The intention would be that at the end of this process all of the members of the group would have the correct understanding of these different forms of business. As a group, they could then work with a business scenario, such as a description of a local, regional, or national business, and identify what sort of business it was – a sole trader, a partnership, a private limited company, or a public limited company.

For activities like this to be effective, you may need to assess learning through questioning. This again, can be differentiated by asking more able learners more probing and difficult questions. However, an alternative approach to questioning could be to plan ahead, write down two or three questions on the board, and provide learners with a set number of minutes to think of a response before selecting learners to provide a response. This is because this creates opportunities for all learners to think about a response, offer a response, albeit basic or incomplete. It avoids the feeling of being under pressure or demotivated, as not all learners can provide a prompt response that is thorough and of a high standard. Allowing thinking time allows learners to think more deeply and provide a more well-thought-out response. Examples of possible questions include:

What is the difference between … and …?
Provide a summary of …
Evaluate the impact on the business as a result of …
Suggest three practical measures the business would need to put in place….

Responses from activities, mini assessments, and effective questioning can allow you to gauge learner understanding through which you can plan further lessons to promote the correct level of progress.

In addition to well-considered and interactive activities, the use of media can be used to make material more memorable to learning, such as well-chosen TV programmes and YouTube clips. In particular, using media that learners can identify with will support their assimilation of the concept, e.g. avoid the use of American material, particularly when key terms can sometimes have different meanings.

Learners also need to be taken out their comfort zone. Stretch and challenge activities are extremely important for students to reach their potential. An example of a challenging activity is:

1 Providing learners with a set of key words/key terms randomly written on a sheet of paper.
2 Ask learners to join up the key terms and write on the line what the relationship between the key terms is.

Well-managed, this can take learners out of their comfort zone, take them into the "struggle zone," which forces them to think, which in turn will enhance learning. (John Hattie and Gregory Yates: *Visible Learning and the Science of How We Learn,* 2014).

In the past, extension activities would be made available for those learners who would complete the learning objectives before the end of the lesson and often became "lesson fillers." To be effective, they must be prepared and available to learners from the beginning of the lesson and can be part of the stretch and challenge strategy within the department. They could be in the form of answering an exam-style question. A more challenging extension activity could be to ask learners to devise a revision quiz for the rest of the group. This could then be used as the plenary. An even more challenging approach is to use a degree standard question for your A level learners. This pushes them beyond the confines of the specification and allows them to consider the demands of Higher Education and how to meet them.

Reflection point:

1 In your opinion what makes a successful lesson?
2 What strategies are you currently using to plan and evaluate a lesson?
3 What strategies are you intending to introduce to your planning now?

Homework

Homework is used for many different reasons: to consolidate learning, review learning, and research to promote independent learning. The homework that you select should contribute towards learner progress, and more importantly, be varied in nature to maintain learner interest. So even though it is to consolidate learning instead of using an exam question or activity out of a textbook, use a current news story that not only informs learners of what is going on in the business world, but allows them to appreciate its context to their learning. For example:

- Select a group of stakeholders who are not happy with the rapid demise of the high street. Discuss why this may be and how they can improve their situation.

OR

- Write a short report of all the business stories you have seen in the news over the past two weeks.

Revision/preparing for exams

Teaching academic subjects brings with it the need to build in some exam preparation, so that learners feel confident and well-prepared for the exam they are about to achieve the qualification through. Learners need revision sessions as some tend to struggle to manage their revision prior to the exam, either through not knowing how to manage all their subjects or through lack of motivation. Furthermore, lack of exposure to exam-style questioning can lead to learners struggling to decipher what the question is asking them, and equally importantly, managing their time to provide a response that is worthy of the high marks within the given time length. This makes revision a fundamentally important part of the teaching and learning cycle.

One of the best revision sessions that I observed had many mini activities that tested learners both individually and in groups. Quick fire rounds and a variety of fast-paced timed activities tested learners' knowledge and challenged them in different ways. Learners were engaged and actively participated in the lesson through which they were able to *enjoy* the act of revision as well as progress with their learning.

Another revision lesson that I thought was equally effective was one that required learners to answer exam-style question under exam conditions. Learners were given the opportunity to discuss the exam question in groups, prepare a plan of how they would structure their response and then they answered the exam question in timed conditions. Once the time was up, if learners needed more time, they were allowed to complete the question as long as they did so in a different coloured pen, so that they were able to realise the speed with which they need to work to be able to fully answer the question in the time allowed. When the question was answered, the teacher then put up the mark scheme on the PowerPoint presentation and talked learners through the mark scheme through which they were able to see what the requirements of the mark scheme were. They first used this to self-assess their responses. They then used a different coloured pen to amend the answer, which would allow them to improve their response. As feedback from these activities is immediate, learners can see the value in them and tend to engage with them more readily. Confirmation of what they are doing right or wrong can be clarified by asking questions and seeking advice from the teacher, which they feel is a better use of their time.

Once activities like this have been mastered by learners, they can be used as independent learning activities. Learners can be given a series of revision questions that can be marked in class, or an exam question for which they can research and plan at home. This exam question can then be completed under exam conditions in the classroom and marked by peers using the mark scheme.

Visits and visitors

As much as you enjoy teaching your learners and they enjoy being in the classroom with you, experiential learning is another approach to providing an excellent learning experience. Learners really appreciate and value being able to make sense of what they have learned/are learning as it adds a different dimension to their learning. A visitor coming into the classroom to discuss his/her own business experiences, including struggles and successes can be more captivating for learners. Learners can ask their questions and investigate the strategies that someone from the world of business adopts on a day-to-day and week-to-week basis. The skills that learners are developing in their written responses to case studies and scenarios become not only academic, but the learners recognise that they are ones that are used in real life.

Another form of experiential learning could be to visit other areas of the school. For example, the Design and Technology (D&T) department can illustrate how Computer-aided Design works in the real world and the benefits and drawbacks of that. The Human Resources, Finance, and Marketing departments can provide learners with an insight into their role in the organisation. This can work well as learners can see how the school or college operates as a business.

A visit out of the classroom can be a bit more complex. It does take a lot more planning and preparation, from selecting the appropriate business or event that will provide the best learning experience, to completing risk assessments, gaining approval for the visit, booking transport and most importantly, devising question sheets that learners can complete while on the external visit to maximise learning. Going into the real world, seeing the locations, the operations and the real people behind the products can provide learners with a hands-on experience that can bring learning to life and provide learners with the motivation they need to engage better with the learning in the classroom, and apply it in the response to the scenarios that they are asked to examine.

Conclusion

Teaching academic subjects can appear to offer the rewards of working with intellectually stimulating subject material and students who are interested and self-motivated. This chapter has shown that there are many different elements to teaching learners studying GCSE and A level subjects and provide examples of approaching the delivery of these subjects with a focus of not only enabling your learners to achieve highly, but also to enjoy their experience of the subject with you as their teacher.

References

Allison, Shaun and Tharby Allison (2015). *Making Every Lesson Count: Six Principles to Support Great Teaching and Learning.* Wales UK: Crown House Publishing Limited.

Berger, Ron (2003). *An Ethic of Excellence: Building a Culture of Craftsmanship with Students.* Portsmouth: Heinemann.

Yates, Gregory C.R. and Hattie, John (2014). *Visible Learning and the Science of How We Learn.* Abingdon, Oxon: Routledge.

Nuthall, Gary (2007). *The Hidden Lives of Learners.* Wellington: NZCER Press.

Further reading

AQA Education GB (online). Available from www.aqa.org.uk [Accessed 21 January 2019]

Assessment Reform Group (1999). *Assessment for Learning - Beyond the Black Box*. Cambridge: University of Cambridge School of Education.

Bostock, John and Wood, Jane. (2012) *Teaching 14–19: A Handbook*. Berkshire: Open University Press.

Capel, Susan Anne; Leask, Marilyn; and Younie, Sarah (2016). *Learning to Teach in the Secondary School: A companion to School Experience*. Abingdon Oxon: Routledge.

Davies, Susan (2006). *The Essential Guide to Teaching*. Harlow: Pearson Education Ltd.

Eduqas (online). Available from www.eduqas.co.uk [Accessed 21 January 2019]

Evans, Carol; Midgley, Alyson; Rigby, Phil; Warham, Lynne; and Woolnough, Peter (2009). *Teaching English*. London: Sage Publications.

Kidd, Warren and Czerniawski, Gerry (2010). *Successful Teaching 14–19, Theory, Practice and Reflection*. London: Sage Publications.

Simmons, Carl and Hawkins, Claire (2015). *Teaching Computing*. London: Sage Publications.

Vygotsky, L. S. (1978). *Mind in Society: The Development of Higher Psychological Processes*. Cambridge, MA: Harvard University Press.

Wallace, Isabella and Kirkman, Leah (2018). *Talk-Less Teaching: Practice, Participation and Progress*. Carmarthen Wales: Crown House Publishing Ltd.

3

GETTING STARTED

Teaching vocational subjects

- Introduction
- The need for reform
- Teaching a vocational course
- Discussion with your mentor – what to ask
- Preparing to teach
- Experiential Learning
- Classroom strategies
- Externally assessed units
- Scheme of work and assessment plan
- Quality assurance processes before and after the production of learner work

  - Assignment brief
  - Verifying learner work

- Conclusion

Introduction

Every teacher recognises the value of vocational education; it provides the teacher with the opportunity to develop in his/her practice of teaching as well as being able to engage with various theories of learning that can inform, develop, and challenge individual practices. For many students coming into teaching, and specifically into the subject area of Business, Economics, and Enterprise, their route has been through the traditional route of A levels and then a degree. While many degrees include vocational elements – and the current emphasis on "employability" within Higher Education means that more University students than ever are expected to engage with Business – teaching on a Level 2 or Level 3 vocational programme for the new teacher is often a completely new, and sometimes overwhelming, experience. Even for those new teachers who have experienced vocational courses before attending University the level of change within this sector of education means that they too have a significant learning journey as they come to grips with the (new) qualification.

Vocational courses provide an excellent pathway for a wide variety of learners. Some learners prefer a more "hands on" approach to learning, in that they prefer to learn through taking part in work–related practical activities while gaining the necessary skills and knowledge for their personal development. This newly gained knowledge is then demonstrated and applied in a piece of written work, which is usually called an "assignment," but it can be in the form of a letter, an advice sheet, or a training booklet. Alternatively, it can be something that is recorded, such as a role-play or presentation which evidences their knowledge and skill acquisition. Sometimes, learners have the option to carry out an activity first in order to meet the learning criteria of a specific unit, for example, organise and hold a fund-raising event, after which they write up a reflection to illustrate their role in the activity and their learning experience of participating in the group activity. Once this individual unit of learning has been completed, learners move on to the next topic, completing another assignment, which is assessed and graded on completion. The final qualification is an aggregation of these individual units of work into an overarching grade, or set of grades.

Another group of learners who are well served through vocational courses are those who have a clear insight of where they want to head in the future. These learners can select a course that is focused on their future interests, is specific to their needs, and relates their learning to the world of work and their future goals and aspirations. Furthermore, for these, as well as all other learners, the wide range of available vocational courses allow the flexibility through which the courses can be studied alongside other vocational and/or academic courses.

As vocational courses that are studied at Level 2 or Level 3 are considered to be equivalent in standard to their GCSE and A level counterparts, learners can tailor-make a learning package that is unique to them by combining a mixture of both vocational and academic courses or by focusing on either vocational or academic routes. Some vocational courses are equivalent to three A Levels, whereas others are equivalent to just one. Therefore, whether learners want to reduce the end-of-course pressure of a full academic course for which they are assessed by sitting for a series of exams at the end of the two years, or would like to learn about a subject that is not available as an academic course, they can create a package combining academic and vocational courses with a progression route that is most suited to them, their learning needs, and their future goals and aspirations.

The wide range of choice within the vocational qualification sector combined with a variety of assessment methods, as well as the use of rigorous quality assurance processes that are not required within traditional academic subjects, means that there are inherent complexities to the planning and delivery of vocational awards. This chapter will provide a background to recent reforms of the vocational qualification sector. Perhaps more importantly, this chapter will also seek to unravel some of the complexities and provide you with a basis to begin your adventure into this stimulating part of the Business, Economics, and Enterprise curriculum. The most commonly used vocational qualifications are for Business. This includes the Business and Technology Education Council (BTEC) suite of qualifications provided by Pearson (https://qualifications.pearson.com/en/subjects/business.html) and the Cambridge Technical qualifications provided by OCR (https://www.ocr.org.uk/subjects/business/). In both cases, the awarding bodies have considerable expertise in the provision of vocational qualifications and are recognised for enabling learners to progress into further and higher education or into employment routes. It is expected that you will familiarise yourself fully with the materials provided by the relevant awarding body as well as use this introduction to the nature of the qualifications.

The need for reform

Despite the benefits that vocational courses provide, they have been heavily criticised over the years, so much so that the focus and commitment to learner progress incited an investigation of vocational courses and the *actual* contribution they make to learner progression in 2010 and 2011. Research entitled *Review of Vocational Education – The Wolf Report* **(March 2011)** highlighted that although many vocational courses provided skills and knowledge at the right level enabling learners to make good progress, some vocational qualifications were not fit for purpose and did not carry any real value. Regardless of this, these poor quality vocational qualifications were still being delivered by schools as performance tables incentivised the school to do so. The assertion was that learners undertaking such courses were being deceived into believing that they were completing a course that was the same in value as a GCSE and provided progression into further education or employment, when in fact they were not, which was morally wrong.

As is the case with many such reports, the headlines that were provided in the press did not carry the full story. For business vocational programmes, there was significant evidence that they provided good progression routes into further and higher education and into employment. As such they were – and continue to be – an important part of our country's educational provision. However, it was clear that overarching reform was needed.

The scrutiny of vocational courses carried out by the *Review of Vocational Education - The Wolf Report* (March 2011) recommended and then ensured that *all* vocational qualifications are rigorous in their teaching, content, and assessment, and made sure that these courses were of relevance to learners and carried credence for educational providers and employers. To ensure rigour, *The Wolf Report* (March 2011) brought with it two significant changes. The first was that the final piece of work should be synoptic, i.e. that it incorporates learning from all previous units so that the learner is required to bring learning forward from all of the other work that has been studied.

The second change has been more controversial. This is the requirement that all vocational courses have an element of external assessment, i.e. exams, should the educational establishment want them to be included in the school/college performance table. For Applied Level 3 courses, this currently accounts for about 40 percent of the whole of the course. Although the externally assessed units on the vocational course bring rigour, they have brought much dissatisfaction from learners, as most embark on a vocational course to avoid the pressures of exams on an academic course. They feel that this new requirement hinders their level of achievement. In addition to this, poor experience of exam-style testing has resulted in lower than expected exam grades and has left learners feeling demoralised with the prospect of having to once again endure the challenges of preparing for exams.

The introduction of exams has also brought additional pressures for tutors. While planning a logical sequence of learning for all qualifications is part and parcel of an effective teacher, the combination of coursework and exam assessments – core and optional units – adds further complexities to the role. The effective teacher has to manage the course to ensure that the core and optional units and the externally assessed exam units are all delivered in a timely fashion whereby they offer learners the best opportunities for success, in addition to following a logical format making relevant links in learning as the course progresses.

Quality-assurance processes for the internally assessed coursework was always a feature of high-quality vocational courses. This continues to be the case with educational establishments requiring a licence to be able to deliver the courses and rigorous internal and external verification procedures. Internal verification occurs within the educational institution, and external means that the verification is undertaken by employees of the exam board. Failure to meet the high standards required results in the licence being revoked.

Despite these challenges, there continue to be many, many good vocational programmes that are highly respected, valuable to employers, and an important part of our country's educational provision. They offer both practical and theoretical content, instil a range of differing skills, and require a variety of teaching and learning strategies, through which learners of all abilities can achieve their goals and aspirations, monitoring their own progress as they go along.

Reflection point:

1 What is your experience of vocational qualifications?
2 What is your perception of the value of vocational qualifications?
3 Does the prospect of delivering such a wide range of assessment models inspire or intimidate you?

Teaching a vocational course

For those who are not familiar with vocational courses, the intricacies of successfully delivering such a course can be difficult to figure out. For such novices, it is worthwhile remembering that there are three aspects of the course that need to be closely managed and monitored to ensure success. They are:

- **Planning** the course by drafting the scheme of work and assessment plan documentation, before the course begins, putting in place the structure and format of the course.
- **Ensuring** that the teaching, learning, and assessment of the course content meet the learning aims and assessment criteria and are within the guided learning hours.
- **Managing** of the verification processes in line to meet standards of quality assurance as directed by the awarding body.

The other key thing to keep in mind is that vocational qualifications are achieved through the completion of a series of *core/mandatory units* and *optional units*. As a vocational qualification, there is an expectation that the exam board developed these by working with both employers and educators, and this is at its most visible within the core units. By definition, core/mandatory (compulsory) units must be completed for the qualification to be achieved. There is a great likelihood that one of the core units is going to be synoptic, ensuring that learners make links with learning from previous units. In addition to this, the points awarded on core/mandatory units are weighted more heavily during the overall grading process. Optional units, on the other hand, provide educational organisations with the freedom to select and focus on a particular vocational area. This will vary from establishment to establishment, depending on the expertise that they have in the department and the progression route they feel is best for their learners.

Assignments produced by learners on these courses are in the main, internally assessed by the teacher, with very tight timelines for feedback. and the assignments are awarded either a Pass, Merit, or Distinction. These individual grades then contribute to the overall achievement of the full award, resulting in anything from a Pass to a Distinction Star. If the qualification is equivalent to more than one GCSE or more than one A level, the final award will reflect that, for example, Merit, Distinction (MD) when the qualification is equivalent to two A levels. The full qualification can only be achieved when a minimum number of units have been completed at a Pass level. Most learners will strive to achieve an overall grade higher than this, as they have the ability to do so.

Just as learners who are completing academic courses, these vocational learners will be required to meet their minimum expected (or target) grade, through which they are able to demonstrate sufficient progress in line with their individual "flight path." Vocational courses allow learners and teachers to monitor this progress quite closely throughout the duration of the course. As units are completed and outcomes are met, the grade achieved per unit can be recorded on a progress tracker. The teacher can then use the progress tracker to monitor the progress of individuals and the group as a whole, and then make appropriate interventions where necessary. This is a huge benefit of vocational courses for the teacher as data monitoring and tracking can be used as an informative, or even a motivational tool through which all stakeholders - learners, parents, teachers, and senior management - are able to see the gradual and real progress that learners are making. Both the learner and the teacher are constantly informed of what is needed to be done so they can achieve their target grades in order to fulfill their future goals and aspirations.

Further assistance is provided through the points allocated to each unit, which can then be used for progression following his/her current level of study. For many University courses, guidance for entry is provided in terms of UCAS points. Learners who wish to progress on to higher education can take the numerical value that they receive for each grade of each completed unit to calculate how many points they have accrued towards the UCAS points needed to gain entry on the course of their chosen University (available on awarding body website). For clarity, many Universities indicate the grades expected for application for a particular course. On a vocational course equivalent to three A levels, the required grade would be Distinction, Distinction, Merit (DDM). This ultimately results in a more focused learner who is familiar with the demands of the course, including the grading outcomes and points allocation. Through this, they are able to take control of their progress and learning, stay on track, and even strive to achieve at a level that is higher than their minimum expected grades. To reinforce this idea of controlling and monitoring their own progress, it is a good idea to ask learners to keep their own personalised tracker, filling in their achievements after each submission so that they are constantly aware of the progress they are making throughout the duration of the course.

With so much of the course being internally assessed, bias is eliminated and quality assurance is maintained through rigorous internal and external verification processes. This includes internal and external verification activities in the form of quality and standardisation checks. Failure to meet the standards of the awarding body can result in the establishment losing its licence to deliver the course, which could leave learners having to re-compile the assignment or even result in without a qualification. This, of course, is not the intention of the awarding body, which is why, on the whole, the awarding bodies provide close links with subject specialists and standards verifiers - who maintain dialogue, offer support and guidance to educational establishments - to ensure that the teaching, learning, assessment, and verification processes are carried out with accuracy so that learners achieve the outcomes they deserve and meet their educational needs. Creating and maintain a positive working relationship with the awarding body is essential, as not only are they a good source of information when it comes to alleviating any queries with regards to the course, but they assist and support with the quality-assurance process, ensuring that rigour is maintained throughout the duration of the course.

Today, there is significant support from online communities and local teacher networks, which will provide guidance and direction. It is common for the awarding body to either set up or be a member of online communities, with the subject specialist stepping in to direct a member to particular resources on their webpage or a person to contact when required.

Discussion with your mentor - what to ask

For the new teacher, there is a lot to take in and absorb when beginning to understand and then deliver a vocational qualification. As well as the website of the relevant qualification, your mentor and the department are significant sources of support. Below are some questions you may want to ask your mentor. The list is long, but it will make a significant difference to your preparations:

- What is the full name of the qualification that I am delivering?
- Which awarding body is it with?
- What is the course code?
- What is the duration of the whole course?
- What is the equivalence of the course to GCSE/A Level course?
- How many exam units are on this course? When are they going to be delivered?
- Which unit will I be teaching on?
- How many sessions a week will I be teaching?
- Will anybody else share the teaching of the course/unit?
- How many sessions a week will they teach?
- Are we going to split a unit or are we going to be teaching individual units?
- Are there any resources connected to the course in the department?
- Where will I find these resources?
- How far have the learners progressed on the course?
- Is there a progress tracker that has been started that I can look at to find out learner progress?
- Where can I find learners' target grades?
- Where is the up-to-date course assessment plan?

- Is there a scheme of work in the department? Where can I find it?
- Has the department organised any trips or visits for the cohort that I will be teaching?
- If so, can I have dates of these?
- Are the learners going to be going on work experience?
- What is the duration of this?
- Do they arrange their own work experience placement, or do we have to help them arrange it?
- Are there any prewritten assignments that I can use to assess my learners?
- Who will internally verify (IV) assignment briefs?
- How much time will they need to internally verify (IV) assignments?
- Who will moderate my work?
- Who is the Lead Internal Verifier (LIV)?
- Where will I find the paperwork for the course?
- Where are all the assignments stored once they have been completed?
- Who can I ask for support in terms of the teaching, learning and, assessment?
- Who is our quality nominee?

Preparing to teach

The questions in the list above are an indication of the amount of research that needs to be carried out prior to teaching a vocational course. Some further research you may wish to carry out to familiarise you with the course and provide you with a holistic view of the qualification that your cohort of learners are working towards could include:

- The number of core units, and what they are.
- The number of optional units, and which ones the department has decided to deliver and why.
- Whether the course has externally assessed units, what they are, when they are likely to be delivered, and when the examination is likely to take place.
- The guided learning hours for each unit on the course, more importantly, the units you are teaching.
- The value of points awarded for the unit you are going to be teaching.
- Who your learners are and where their strengths and weaknesses lie.
- Any behaviour issues with the cohort of learners.
- Any sensitive information you need to be aware of in relation to your learners.

Having an in-depth knowledge of your learners, as well as the course itself, can allow you to consider things such as pace, strategies for learning activities, target setting, and interleaving with previous units of learning and, forward teaching by making links with upcoming units of learning. Not only are these important for progress, but they prompt learners to think beyond the learning that is presently taking place. In addition to this, awareness of the learning aims is important in ensuring that what is being taught is relevant and delivered at the appropriate level during the time permitted through which learners apply and display newly acquired knowledge to meet the demands of the assignment.

High-quality teaching, learning, and assessment are vital as the limited number of guided learning hours per unit means that learners have few opportunities to recap and review learning before they are allocated the assignment which, in essence, provides the evidence of the level of skill and knowledge they have acquired. This means that differentiation, stretch and challenge, and regular assessment must be implemented in the learning process in the same way as if you were teaching an academic subject. It is important to remember that as with any other subject, or any other group, there will be learners of varying abilities in your group. As a teacher, it is your responsibility to ensure that *all* learners are able to effectively access the learning material and gain familiarity with it so that they are able to demonstrate their understanding of the topic.

In order to accelerate learning and to empower learners, strategies such as those discussed in Chapter 2 "Getting Started: Teaching Academic Subjects," could be used, including a combination of paired and group activities through which they can clarify their learning with each other. This is a good strategy to use as the learners build on their team working and communication skills while learning with each other. Asking learners to present their findings to the rest of the group can further instill confidence in learners. Engaging learning activities that encourage active participation could include mix-and-match activities, solving word puzzles, unscrambling sentences, or completing word banks, particularly at Level 2. These activities can be successful as learners independently interact with the learning material, draw inferences from it, and actually study at depth. Additionally, using a wide variety of activities can assist in ensuring that the learning needs of a wide range of learners are met, and provide them with ways to participate in the lesson and develop their knowledge.

Resources that are up to date and which learners can relate to can escalate learning and are evidence of high-quality teaching for the Business, Economics, and Enterprise specialist. For example, using news articles about the battle of Nestle to keep the design of Kit Kat®, their four-fingered snack, protected and unique to themselves can inform learners of what a registered trademark is and generate lively discussion and debate. When resources used in classroom activities include items from everyday life, they provide learners with a way to make connections between the real world and the classroom, thus making learning purposeful (*The Process of Education*, Jerome Bruner, 1960). Moreover, having a broad knowledge base equips learners well, as they are better informed and they are better able to articulate themselves on paper providing a developed response, which is of a high level. Resources that you may use should be checked for (English) spelling, grammar, and punctuation, as well as how the information on the resource is presented to instill good standards of literacy skills in learners.

Learners should also be encouraged to keep all classwork and independent work in an organised file so that they can refer to it to produce a response that is truly reflective of what they have learnt; this, in effect, negates the temptation to plagiarise. The more confident learners are with their newly acquired knowledge, the more likely they are to express themselves in their own words and in their own style, and to provide a genuine piece of work. This is opposed to looking for an easy way out by replicating or "copying and pasting" information off the Internet that does not sound like them and leaves them with a piece of work that they cannot relate to at all. The benefits of learners enjoying their learning experience and working towards creating a genuine piece of work is more likely to result in them producing material that they can remember and apply to a variety of situations. Moreover, learners need to recognise the ethical implications of plagiarised work as a form of intellectual theft that carries penalties.

Even with the highest level of learning, some learners may not feel prepared to go away and independently produce a piece of work that is going to be assessed and contribute to their final grade. To assist learners in achieving this skill, preparatory activities could include providing learners with a range of tasks or scenarios similar to those they could be expected to complete as part of their assignment. These could be completed in pairs or as grouped activities so that learners can lean on each other's skills and knowledge in order to gain the highest grade possible. To maximise learning and differentiate, a scaffold-containing a series of questions focusing learners' attention on key pieces of information through which they could meet the assessment criteria - could also be provided to support learners so they could write a suitable response. Using these "shadow scenarios" is similar to using past paper questions to prepare learners for an exam on an academic course. As such, they are excellent preparation in preparing your learners to gain familiarisation with, and meet the needs of, the assessment criteria. Activities such as these are vital in enabling learners to demonstrate their understanding and identify areas of weakness that they may need clarification on, and research further, so that they could make good progress.

As learners are fully focused on completing their assignment they often feel that using such strategies, and theory lessons themselves, are a waste of their precious time. They just want to receive their assignment so that they can begin working on it. However, as the level of support that learners are provided during the writing of the assignment is minimal - to reflect the exam expectations of their academic counterparts - this eagerness needs to be reined in so that learners make good use of the allocated learning time in order to develop the appropriate skill and knowledge acquisition that can be reflected in the assignment they produce.

Experiential Learning

Experiential Learning plays a key role in vocational education, not only because of its holistic nature but because, as David A Kolb explains, knowledge is acquired from the combination of "grasping and transforming experience." (David A Kolb, 1984: 41) which, in essence, is the purpose of vocational education. Learners expect to participate in work-related activities through which they gain skills and knowledge that not only contributes to their qualification but to their wider experience. The range of methods of learning experientially is broad, including:

- Tasters (visiting speaker or visit to the organisation)
- Simulation (equivalent to what happens in business, but not engaging with real customers)
- Live brief (engaging with real customers; which may be set by a business and with the possibility of results being adopted by the business)
- Work experience
- Internships
- Working with employers and/or employer panels in the development of the qualification.

Much will depend on what the school or college expects from the delivery of vocational qualifications and an awareness of what is available for learners.

In schools and colleges, learners develop practical skills mainly through business simulations, whereby they participate in activities such as role plays and presentations within the classroom. Outside of the classroom, learners may be asked to participate in a live brief, such as organising an event to fundraise, such as a car wash or end-of-term disco. These activities create an environment where learners can reflect on their strengths and weaknesses, as well as what they feel the key learning points of the experience are.

To gain first-hand experience of the world of work, learners should embark on a period of work experience with a business organisation. This snapshot of experience, which could be for a period of up to two weeks, requires learners to arrive at work wearing appropriate dress for the organisation and carrying out daily activities alongside established staff members who are employed by the business organisation. The benefits of this are vast; learners are afforded the opportunity to converse with and follow instructions from people other than their parents or teachers. Learners can reflect on the different types of people they may find themselves working with in the future. In addition to this, they may realise the types of sanctions that employees face in the real world, such as if they are late, if they are not wearing the correct uniform, or if they don't complete allocated tasks in the time length suggested by the manager. Experience has shown that this can be significant in the development of learners as they perceive the connection between their classroom-based learning and the business environment – and the implications of successful completion of their qualification.

It is important to visit learners when they are in this environment, so you can see how differently they behave away from school or college. Some learners may be more mature, respectful and confident; others may feel vulnerable away from the school or college environment and appear shy and reserved. Your visit not only gives learners some sense of security but allows them to speak to you about the connections they have been able to make between school/college and working life, and the learning points about their individual experience. For further reflection, learners could be provided with a booklet they could fill out during the work experience so that they could record their thoughts and feelings while they are fresh in their minds.

As well as being a learning experience for learners, visiting them at work provides you with an opportunity to enhance your own understanding of how (local) businesses function. This can be used to enhance learner experience when back in school or college by making the connections between their thoughts and feelings of their experience and theory and practice, bringing the subject to life.

Arranging learner visits to local businesses or inviting members of the local business community to come and speak to your cohort can further enhance experiential learning. Real decisions that businesses have had to make to reach the level of success they are experiencing intrigues learners and gives them an insight into the highs and lows of the business world. Visits to local and national businesses provide learners with a sense of how businesses are structured, how they operate, and the significance of each job role in the smooth running and success of the organisation. To get the most out of these learning experiences, it is important to liaise with the business beforehand to organise the focus of learning as well as provide fact-finding sheets for learners that they can complete during the visit, recording vital information that is of relevance to them and their learning and development.

When organising work experience visits or a visit to a business or a speaker it is important to consider the benefits to the business for doing this. It may be a case of fitting into a business model of Corporate Social Responsibility, or a way of the business gaining insight into the skills of local young people. Another potential benefit, rarely used, is the possibility of training for their own workforce through the creation of a simulation for their own staff and visiting learners to work through.

At the start of this section, internships and engagement with employer panels were also mentioned. While they may not fall within the remit of the qualification, the work of Enabling Enterprise (http://enablingenterprise.org/) and My Kinda Future (www.mykindafuture.com) have both led to an increase in ways for learners to enhance their experience of working with businesses. Some of these can be linked to specific elements of the qualification, or to enhance the wider experience of learners.

Each of these approaches have their unique place in the learning cycle of learners. Although setting up a broad range of experiences takes time – and school and college processes need to be followed – allowing learners to learn from such experiences is vital to their development on the course and as young adults.

Reflection point:

The next section investigates a range of strategies to enable teaching on a vocational course to be effective. In preparation for this, consider the following questions:

1 What makes a successful lesson?
2 What has been your experience of teaching on vocational programmes?
3 What strategies have you seen that allow for learners to develop their skills of self-regulation and meta-cognition?

Classroom strategies

A common approach to the delivery of a vocational qualification is for each unit to be delivered independently. Within the unit delivery, the content is often delivered as a block of teaching at the start. After this initial teaching, the assignment is distributed with a deadline that marks the amount of time learners have to complete the assignment. Sadly, it is not unusual for learners to conclude that all that they need to do for each lesson is to come to class and sit at a computer until the end of the lesson. Inevitably, this leads learners to make limited progress and it is the most common reason for behaviour issues on vocational courses. Together, these contribute heavily to vocational courses receiving bad press.

Research has shown that a vocational course can incorporate as much creativity and learner progression as any other qualification (Helena Knapton and Jill McKenzie, 2016). Some of the strategies that you could use to limit disruption and encourage learner progress are as follows:

- The most obvious strategy is the use of a lesson structure that incorporates learning objectives, an appropriate introduction to these at the start (activity, discussion, etc.) and a review of learning against those learning objectives during and at the end of the lesson. The way in which learning objectives are developed will vary according to the motivation and ability of learners as well as the assignment variety and challenge. With some groups, you will find that learners will be able to identify their own learning objectives; for others, greater direction from you as the teacher will be required.

- When handing out the assignment, discuss the individual criteria elements with learners, ensuring that they have a good understanding of what the criteria demands. Signpost them to when and where the learning took place. This knowledge will assist them in completing those particular criteria. Encourage learners to make a note of this on their assignment sheet so that they always have this direction available to them. This will help to avoid the sense of lack of direction they may feel in having to complete the assignment without the teacher to lean on.

- To provide an element of interleaving with previous learning, you could discuss similar activities that learners have completed in which they have addressed these criteria before, for example, the "shadow scenarios" they may have completed. Again, this could be something they could make a note of on their assignment sheet to help trigger their memory. This important strategy is helpful not just to learners in allowing them to make the connection between what they have learnt and the application of it, but it helps build confidence. Learners can recognise that they have acquired the knowledge and skills needed to achieve the assessment criteria, adequately responding to the command words and providing the depth of response that is required within the expected time frame.

- Together these can be used by learners to create their own scheme of work, identifying when and how they will meet each of the criteria. This is an important development of their own skills of self-regulation, which is such an important factor in success both for an individual qualification and for their future career.

- Awareness of the task in hand means that learners can break down the assignment into manageable chunks. This enables learners to set their own timeline of activities so that they are able to meet the demands of the assignment at the appropriate level and within the given deadlines. This strategy enables all learners to stay on track with the completion of the assignment, so that if they have an absence, they know what they have to do to catch up. In addition to this, if learners are all completing similar activities, albeit at different levels, this strategy means that the teacher can manage the beginning of lessons by developing activities that will help to focus learners' minds on what they will be working on for the rest of the lesson, and act as triggers, helping learners to recall key terms and knowledge relevant to the assignment. This not only leads to a smooth start to the lesson but gives learners a sense of purpose in doing teacher-directed work.

- At various staging points (which may be each lesson) learners can engage in their own self-review of learning. This is done by learners checking that their individual work meets each of the criteria and in accordance to their timescale identified in their original planning. Building in provision for learners to step back and undertake this self-review develops the meta-cognition skills of learners. This is because it promotes the skill of learners to interrogate what they have done and digest what they have to do, in the time they have available. Thus, this focusses learners' minds on the task in hand.

- Helena Knapton and Jill McKenzie (2016) recommend another activity that can be used at the beginning of the lesson that will help learners to stay focussed on their work; it requires a little preparation. Learners are provided with a proforma for learners to write down their targets for the session and identify how they would achieve these targets. Learners should provide at least three targets per lesson. At key points during the lesson, learners can self-review their own progress.
- A further version of this includes the use of a set of laminated discs. For each of the targets, learners are provided a laminated disc. These could be anything. They could resemble traffic lights, hence:

  - *Red* would indicate the first target.
  - *Orange* would indicate that the learner is working on the second target.
  - *Green* would indicate that the learner is working on the third target.

An alternative could be bronze, silver, and gold medals, or they could even be different modes of transport. You can be as creative as you like with these laminated stickers. They are merely indicators that learners will place on the corner of their monitor to indicate which target they are working on. This simple strategy means that you can stand at a single point in the classroom and know exactly where each learner is up to, manage behaviour, and monitor progress. Where learners are not making progress, it is easier to target those learners and address the issue of poor progress with them. This strategy further assists in a smooth ending to the lesson, whereby learners spend the last 5 to 10 minutes of the lesson reflecting on the level of progress that they have made and what it was that helped or hindered their progress. Through this, learners can begin to think about the next lesson and the targets they may need to set for themselves. This could be something as simple as managing their own behaviour. But it could be recognising that progress was not as swift as they had hoped because they are struggling to articulate their knowledge and what they know into an adequate response to the assignment. This then encourages learners to spend more time carrying out independent reading around the topic or revisiting their notes and any other previous work to find a solution of how they can overcome this barrier to their progress.

These methods of delivering vocational lessons contribute well to learner progress and create a learning experience from which learners become aware of their limitations, recognise their strengths, track and monitor their personal progress, reflect on these, and improve their work ethic. Together these are skills of both meta-cognition (understanding how they learn) and self-regulation (managing how they learn). These skills not only allow learners to progress with their work while on this course. It further enables them to become independent learners who know how to set targets for themselves and find the correct working conditions in which they can learn independently and complete their work within given deadlines. As this method requires learners to reflect at the end of every lesson, they are less likely to have an excuse for not completing the assignment on the hand in date.

Another aspect of learner work that causes much frustration for tutors is the constant issue of "lost work." Either learners lose their USB pens or that they have not saved their work correctly, making it impossible to retrieve. To avoid issues like this, create an on-line classroom, enroll learners to the class, and ask learners to complete their work on this on-line class. Learners can create whatever documents they need to on this online platform and complete their work there. Not only does this mean that learner work is less likely to "mysteriously disappear," but learner performance can be monitored in a variety of ways.

Monitoring learner performance can include ensuring that the work is not plagiarised. Work that is submitted electronically is easier to check for plagiarism and easier to verify for the meeting of deadlines. Where plagiarism is detected, the evidence can be presented to learners and sanctions issued per the awarding body guidelines. The fact that an online platform is being used for the monitoring of learner work acts as an immediate deterrent from the temptation of learners to copy and paste huge swathes of information from the Internet and try to pass the information as their own. This is because learners are all too aware of the ease with which plagiarism can be detected and the consequent impact on their progression.

Electronic platforms display dates and times of when they were visited by learners. Therefore, those learners who make poor progress have fewer places to hide and there is a tighter monitoring of progress. This can be checking the completion of tasks, or time spent independently completing homework, and the duration of that. Another advantage for the teacher of using an electronic platform is the access to learner work for the purposes of assessment. As the teacher, you are expected to create and control your own assessment plan. This not only supports teacher autonomy - important for your own well-being - but it can be used to identify and provide support for those learners who are lagging behind.

These online platforms add an additional dimension to learner progress. Learners come to appreciate and experience a different kind of learning that is synonymous with learning in further and higher education institutions, and in future commercial contexts, thereby preparing them for a more independent and mature approach to learning.

Externally assessed units

As mentioned earlier, *Review of Vocational Education - The Wolf Report* (2011) recommended that all vocational courses should now contain externally assessed units. For success on this part of the course, strategies suggested in Chapter 2 "Getting Started: Teaching Academic Subjects" should be used. However, even before this, you can carry out research to find out the availability of exams with the exam board. Using that, balance out the teaching and learning of the externally assessed units with the internally assessed units so that learners do not feel too much pressure with regards to the exams. This advanced planning will further allow you to provide learners with the benefit of re-sit opportunities that are available to help them to achieve their desired target grade.

Scheme of work and assessment plan

Two of the most important documents that you need for the delivery of a vocational programme are the **scheme of work** and the **assessment plan**. Both of these are important in the planning process, ensuring that you remain within the given time-lines of the course. The scheme of work will provide you with information about the units themselves, aspects of the unit that you need to deliver, how they are broken down, how much time you need to spend on each criteria, which aspect of the course specification they are relevant to, which aspect they are interlinked with and which assessment criteria of the assignment can be used to assess the learning of the scheme of work. Completed well, your scheme of work can be your one single document that you call upon to ensure you are on track with the teaching and learning of the course. A scheme of work is described as a "working document," which means that it is not set in stone, but is one that can be adapted according to your experience as the teacher, the progress that learners make, and in response to external factors, all within the necessary parameters of the assessment requirements of the qualification, which are externally set.

Developing the scheme of work is an invaluable skill as vocational courses have several pieces of documentation that constantly need to be referred to, namely the **assessment criteria** and the **learning aims document.** Using these when developing the scheme of work will help you to maintain consistency and pace, and ensure you are on the right track in terms of meeting the assessment criteria. In addition to this, use these documents to monitor the progress of learners on the course, ensuring that they complete with the highest possible grade in the required time to receive the accreditation in the correct academic year so that they can progress onto their next level of learning.

An example of a scheme of work has been provided in Chapter 2 "Getting Started: Teaching Academic Subjects." The scheme of work produced for a vocational qualification will follow a similar approach. What is significantly different, however, is the necessity of ensuring that it is integrated with the assessment plan, which will identify the key dates for assignments to be completed and exams to be sat in accordance with the examining board requirements.

The importance of the assessment plan is that it allows you to monitor when an assignment needs to be allocated to learners, when the submission date needs to be set for, and when assignments need to be marked and returned to learners so that they have sufficient time to correct the work in the allocated time for resubmission. Figure 3.1 shows an example of an assessment plan. The option for resubmission is a great benefit for learners, but it brings huge pressures on teachers. The short time frame in which the assignments need to be marked according to the assessment plan can be quite stressful, especially if there are large cohorts. To maintain integrity in the assessment process, not only do the assignments need to be marked, they need to be internally verified too so that the marking can be agreed upon with either another member of the staff who has experience of assessing at this level or the lead Internal Verifier (IV) within the school/college.

As with the scheme of work, the assessment plan is a working document that can be annotated with changes as the year progresses. This is to inform you of how your practice is likely to evolve as the year develops. It is absolutely vital that both of these documents are annotated or adjusted to provide a true and up-to-date picture of the progress of the course. The reason for this is that you can monitor how the course is progressing, through which you can gain a realistic insight of how much time is being spent on each individual unit so that one or two units do not dominate too much time, leaving learners at risk of not receiving the number of guided learning hours for the other units of learning. Just as learners need to self-regulate their learning, so do you as a teacher. There is always a necessity to reflect on the development of the programme of learning, to consider how learners respond to the ways in which you deliver the course, and to be able to review your own strengths and areas for development.

As indicated earlier, there are stringent quality-assurance processes in place to protect the credibility of the qualification, particularly following *Review of Vocational Education - The Wolf Report* (2011) and government response to this. One aspect of this is the *external verification process*, which is undertaken by employees (External Verifiers)

BTEC assessment plan

Programme number & title   **Level 2 First award in Business**

Unit No & Title	Assignment No & Title	Assessment Criteria	Available on VLE from	Hand In Date	IV Sampling Date	Resubmission Date	Resubmission IV Sampling Date	Assessor Name	IV Name
Unit 3 Promoting a Brand	Branding and Promotion	P1 P2 P3 M1 M2 D1	17/10/2018	12/11/2018	30/11/2018	10/12/2018	20/12/2018	JG	SD
Unit 3 Promoting a brand	Developing and Promoting My Brand	P4, P5, M3, M4 D2	12/11/2018	07/12/2018	19/12/2018	09/01/2019	23/01/2019	JG	SD

Figure 3.1 Example of an assessment plan.

of the exam board. When the external verification process is due to take place the first thing that the External Verifier will ask for is the assessment plan. This, along with the grade tracker, is used to select the units and a selection of learners to be involved in the external verification process. If the assessor has a true picture of the course, the report that he/she provides is likely to be a true reflection of the practices adopted by the department, supporting the department in their delivery of learning, assessment, and overall organisation of the course. Therefore, it is extremely important that both the assessment plan and the data tracker are kept updated.

Quality assurance processes before and after the production of learner work

Assignment brief

Learners demonstrate their learning through the completion of an assignment. Each assignment must be internally verified by another member of the teaching team in the department, or the Lead Internal Verifier (LIV) within the school or college, prior to it being distributed to the learners for completion. This is an essential part of the quality-assurance process. It must be completed in a timely fashion to ensure that the assignment is fit for purpose, meets the assessment criteria, and is rigorous in the level of assessment. Each of these is important in ensuring that the tasks set in the assignment are challenging yet achievable and meet the needs of the assessment criteria, without which learners may not achieve their qualification. For those who may find themselves as the only member of the school (or college) delivering a vocational qualification from that exam board, support is provided by the exam board to ensure that the necessary checks and balances are in place.

The quality-assurance procedure further checks if the paperwork on which learners are allocated the assignment has the correct course code, course title, dates, and assessor details. Although these things may seem trivial, they contribute towards the validity and authentication of the assessment. The assessor, in effect, places his/her signature on the document to authenticate that the learner has achieved the criteria awarded, which is as stated on the documentation. In addition, the learner provides his/her signature to authenticate their work. Without learner and assessor signatures, the accreditation of the unit - and therefore the qualification - simply will not be awarded.

Verifying learner work

Once learner work is completed, it must be marked and verified as per the quality assurance procedure prior to it being returned to learners to view, amend, and following resubmission (if required), marked once more. It is then stored securely, on site, in a locked place for the length of time as stated by the awarding body. This is often for the duration of a year or so, some awarding bodies suggest that merely the paperwork which evidences the verification process needs to be kept for three years, yet learner work can be returned after 3 months.

When marking learner work, the quality assurance procedure and best practices dictate that the feedback must reflect the wording as stated in the assessment criteria. This is so that learners can clearly see what they have achieved and the extent to which this achievement meets the needs of the criteria. Consistently using such language, for the purpose of feedback, will allow learners to recognise what they need to do to achieve the criteria if improvements are needed. This is of great importance as not only does this provide consistency in the feedback that learners receive, but rigour is provided by adhering to the standards as provided by the awarding body. This includes not providing learners with excessive amounts of support or direction through which they are able to vastly improve their submission and achieve the criteria. This again is important for the purposes of quality assurance and time must be spent in familiarising yourself with what is acceptable. For this, you can seek advice from the awarding body website. Alternatively, you can look at the feedback that has been provided by other, more-experienced members of staff to see the wording that has been used. Alternatively, a sample of marked work could be passed to the Lead Internal Verifier (LIV), or anyone else responsible for the quality-assurance procedure so that they can vet it against the assessment criteria and advise you on whether or not the marking and feedback is of the correct standard, *and* is likely to meet the requirements of the quality-assurance procedure. It is important that such measures are taken to help thwart the temptation to provide learners with too much of a clear direction of what needs to be done through which the assessment criteria can be met. If learners are provided with more assistance than that suggested by the exam board this can lead to their accreditation being withdrawn.

Once learner work is assessed by yourself, the quality assurance procedure needs to be followed and the internal verification process must be completed. This must be done as soon as each assignment is submitted, selecting work from a range of learners to further illustrate fairness and authenticity. The Lead IV, or another member of staff from the department will check standards of assessment, and either agree or disagree with your awarding decisions providing you with their reasons for their view. The Lead IV will complete and sign relevant paperwork to authenticate this process. This is an essential part of the verification process and must be completed properly at the time. This is because without relevant signatures on the appropriate paperwork the authentication process can be deemed as invalid, leaving the educational establishment at risk of losing their accreditation to deliver the award and the learner at risk of not receiving their award.

If learners do not meet the demands of each of the assessment criteria, they may be given the permission to resubmit their work. Once again, the appropriate paperwork must be completed to meet the standards of the quality-assurance procedure.

The final part of the quality-assurance procedure involves the External Verifier (EV) and the standardisation visit. This is critical in receiving confirmation from the exam board that the processes adopted by the educational establishment in relation to validity and authenticity are at the correct standard as prescribed by the exam board. Keeping all documentation completed and up to date is an integral part of this process, reiterating the importance of ensuring that this aspect of the course is thoroughly completed.

Conclusion

Although delivering vocational qualifications includes a variety of challenges, they continue to be popular with schools and colleges. This is not only because it provides learners with the possibility of progressing into further and higher education, or into employment but because they provide learners with the opportunity to enjoy their learning, to make connections between their lives outside of school or college and more academic endeavours, and for some students, to have their skills, abilities, and achievements formally recognised in a way that traditional academic endeavours cannot provide. The changes that have been introduced following the *Review of Vocational Education - The Wolf Report* (2011) has not only led to an increase in rigour for the qualifications, but also ensured that they continue to have credibility and are appropriate for our modern-day context.

References and recommended reading

Bruner, Jerome. (1960). *The Process of Education*. Cambridge, MA: Harvard University Press.

BTEC Business Qualifications (2019). Pearson (online) Available from: https://qualifications.pearson.com/en/subjects/business.html [Accessed 8 April 2019]

Cambridge Technical Business Qualifications (2019). OCR (online) Available from: https://www.ocr.org.uk/subjects/business/ [Accessed 8 April 2019]

Harrison, Angela. (2011). Vocational Education Not Good Enough Says Wolf Report. London. BBC (online) Available from: https://www.bbc.co.uk/news/education-12622061 [Accessed 8 April 2019]

Knapton, Helena and McKenzie, Jill (2016). "The Secret of Engaging and Effective Coursework Lessons!" *Teaching Business & Economics* (The Economics, Business, and Enterprise Association), 20 (3) pp. 4–7.

Kolb, David A. (1984). *Experiential Learning: Experience as the Source of Learning and Development*. Englewood Cliffs, NJ: Prentice Hall.

Molloy, David (2018). Kit Kat® Case: No Break for Nestlé in Trademark Row. London. BBC (online) Available from: https://www.bbc.co.uk/news/world-europe-44939819 [Accessed 8 April 2019]

Quigley, Alex; Muijs, Daniel; and Stringer, Eleanor (2019). Metacognition and Self-Regulated Learning Guidance Report, Education Endowment Foundation. London (online). Available from: https://educationendowmentfoundation.org.uk/public/files/Publications/Metacognition/EEF_Metacognition_and_self-regulated_learning.pdf [Accessed 8 April 2019]

Wallace, Isabella and Kirkman, Leah (2018). *Talk-Less Teaching: Practice, Participation and Progress*. Carmarthen Wales: Crown House Publishing Ltd.

Wolf, Alison (2011). Review of Vocational Education - The Wolf Report. London. Department for Education (online). Available from: https://assets.publishing.service.gov.uk/government/uploads/system/uploads/attachment_data/file/180504/DFE-00031-2011.pdf [Accessed 21 January 2019]

4

LEARNING AND TEACHING STRATEGIES

Assessment for Learning

- An introduction to Assessment for Learning
- Assessment for Learning – where it started; what it means
- Where to start – finding out what your learners know
- Learning theory
- Sharing objectives and working with success criteria
- "In Lesson" Assessment for Learning approaches and strategies
- Assessment of enterprise and/or work-related learning
- Challenges – and how to manage them
- Linking Assessment for Learning (AfL) to differentiation
- Conclusion

An introduction to Assessment for Learning

There is a story that can be found in a number of different places of a man in the pub – let's call him Joe – talking to his friend, Fred, who says, "I taught my dog to whistle." Hearing this Fred replies, "But your dog can't whistle." "I never said he had learnt," says Joe.

Teaching and learning is a complex activity and both research and experience has shown that for learner learning to be effective then teaching cannot be a case of the teacher doing something at the front of the class and hoping that learners pick up what is being taught. The role of the teacher must be much more reflexive than that – finding out what learners know and what they can do. The teacher then has to be able to adapt their teaching to enable the learners to add to their knowledge and skills in subsequent lessons. The process of gaining and using the evidence of learner learning as they progress through a course of learning is called **Assessment *for* Learning**. As staff gather that evidence then they can plan future lessons with confidence that they are meeting their learner needs and that learners are more likely to be successful in the future. The activities that allow for assessment for learning to take place are described as **formative assessment.**

Implementing Assessment for Learning into your lessons can be a powerful tool for enhancing learner progress within lessons and across a course. Many schools have their own policies and procedures, some of which are not automatically transferable between schools. Understanding the principles that underpin those strategies is, therefore, important to allow for practice to be adapted for different contexts. Consequently, within this chapter we will be looking at those principles as well as how they can be translated into strategies.

There is another form of assessment, which is called **summative assessment.** This comes at the end of a course of learning, for example, the GCSE (General Certificate in Secondary Education) grade or a BTEC (Business and Technology Education Council) qualification, or at the end of the module. Sometimes it is described as a summary of learning. At this point in time, summative assessment is the main method of identifying whether or not the teacher has been successful in managing the learning of their learners as well as being a summary of learner achievement.

This focus on summative assessment as being a way of assessing the capability of staff, and of the school, has resulted in many teachers "teaching to the test." In other words, the teaching in lessons is almost wholly focused on the development of specification knowledge and exam skills, thereby limiting the breadth of learner experience and wider learning of the subject. Taking this approach may alleviate concerns about learner progress, but doing so often reduces job satisfaction and therefore motivation of both staff and learners. By being able to analyse the effectiveness of the assessment methods that you choose to use you can be empowered to assess in a way that will enable your learners to take responsibility for their own learning and to ensure that you are not adding to their workload or to your own unnecessarily.

This chapter is, therefore, ambitious in its intentions. The aim is to enable you to have a deep understanding of assessment for learning so that you can use this to enable your learners to make good or better progress and to enjoy their learning – and for you to enjoy your teaching.

Assessment for Learning – where it started; what it means

Good teachers have always assessed learner learning and provided constructive feedback to help learners to achieve more. However, it was only as a result of the publication of *Inside the Black Box: Raising Standards through Classroom Assessment* by Paul Black and Dylan Wiliam, in 1998, did the significance of formative assessment start to become widely known and an expectation that all teachers use assessment as a tool to develop learner learning. As a result of this work the Assessment Reform Group was set up and they identified key principles of Assessment for Learning (AfL). As well as being integral to classroom practice, the principles identified that AfL should be motivational, focused on learner learning (progress), promote learner understanding of goals and success criteria, and enable learners to know how to improve and develop learner capacity for self-assessment.

In 2008, the Department for Children, Schools and Families developed *The Assessment for Learning Strategy* to be implemented into every school with these aims:

- **every child** knows how they are doing and understands what they need to do to improve and how to get there. They get the support they need to be motivated, independent learners on an ambitious trajectory of improvement;

- **every teacher** is equipped to make well-founded judgements about pupils' attainment, understands the concepts and principles of progression, and knows how to use their assessment judgements to forward plan, particularly for learners who are not fulfilling their potential;
- **every school** has in place structured and systematic assessment systems for making regular, useful, manageable and accurate assessments of pupils, and for tracking their progress;
- **every parent and carer** knows how their child is doing, what they need to do to improve, and how they can support the child and their teachers.

While this strategy no longer exists, every school and every teacher would recognise that these reflect current expectations on teachers and learners. They would also identify that the place of data has increased with schools using sophisticated data management systems and with external bodies (i.e. Ofsted) using learner achievement data to make comparisons between learners within the school and against national benchmarked data. Examples of the types of comparisons that are routinely made are according to student background (disadvantaged or not), gender, term of birth, ethnic background, whether or not English is their first language, and free school meals. What is important to know is that data or student tracking is NOT assessment for learning. Being able to use that data to inform teaching and to support student learning is what transforms this into assessment for learning.

Where to start – finding out what your learners know

Research shows that Assessment for Learning is at its most powerful when it enables the teacher to know what is in the mind of their learners at the start of their teaching so as to be able to scaffold learning effectively. That teaching could be at the start of a course, a topic, or a lesson. There are a number of different approaches to identify what your learners know; when and how these approaches are used will vary widely. For example, when learners are new to the topic, to the subject, or to the level of study or school/college, it can be appropriate to be quite formal in the approach taken in order to understand not only what learners know but also the skills that they have to be able to manage the material. However, within individual lessons more informal approaches may be used to find out how their understanding is progressing and if there are any misconceptions to be addressed.

An example of when **formal, diagnostic testing** of learners takes place can be found in some schools within a socially deprived area where they identify the reading age of their learners at the start of their GCSE study, as well as at Year 6 through the Statutory Assessment Tests (SATs) in preparation for the start of secondary school. For Business teachers, this is very important so that they can ensure that they work with their learners to build their technical language of the subject and of the assessment criteria of the specification and the materials to be used in the exams. Addressing this is not merely a case of "teaching to the test," but also providing wider literacy skills that will support them as they progress into post-16 contexts.

Diagnostic testing can also take place at the start of Level 3 qualifications to find out not only what the learners know but also their ability to manipulate information, write clearly, and to find out to what extent they are able to analyse and evaluate. This may be less formal than assessing a learner's reading age and more specifically tailored to the subject and qualification. For those teaching within the post-16 sector where new learners come from different schools, this process is particularly important. The types of diagnostic assessment can be through individual tutorials with learners or by undertaking a written task that requires learners to be able to show that they can respond to written stimulus material by interrogating the information and writing an appropriate response. Such diagnostic testing will sit alongside the information that will be made available from the earlier formal, summative assessment that comes from GCSE results.

The formal, summative assessment that comes from GCSE results is also used to identify what grades learners are most likely to achieve at the end of post-16 study through the availability of national benchmark data. Most schools and colleges then use this information to provide learners with a "minimum target grade" and staff assess learner progress against this benchmark data. However, the most common, and perhaps important, form of formal, summative assessment that is used to assess the quality of learner progress comes from the SATs that learners sit at the end of Key Stage 2, in year 6. Based on the information provided from Year 6 SATs, national benchmark data is used to indicate what grades at GCSE these learners will achieve. The success of the school (and of individual teachers) is then determined by the achievement of learners against this benchmark data. While the individual business teacher may argue that the assessment criteria for SATs at Key Stage 2 has little or no similarity with what is being assessed within a GCSE Business or BTEC Level 2 qualification, there is still value in identifying what learners could do at the end of year 6 and how they have continued to develop (or make progress) since then. Therefore, taking the time to see learners in Key Stage 3 classes is important both for the new teacher and for the updating of a teacher. This understanding can then be used to inform the teachers' planning and expectations of their learners within their daily teaching.

Having identified where learners have come from will enable school staff to plan individual lessons across a period of time so that material is scaffolded in a way that ensures that learners are ready for the next round of national exams (summative assessments). It is important that there will be opportunities for the teacher to formally assess what progress each learner is making against the learning intentions of that lesson (also known as "learning objectives" or even "learning outcomes"). To do this a **formal teacher assessment** will be done at the end of each learning intention to ensure that every learner has been able to achieve that learning intention at a level appropriate for that learner.

While the assessment strategy within an individual lesson will have these identified stopping points to assess to what extent learners are making progress, there will also be an **informal teacher assessment** done to assess progress as the teacher delivers that learning intention. A simple example is when a task is set and it becomes clear that learners don't understand exactly what is required of them. The teacher will find that learners are asking him/her the same question repeatedly, or that many learners are not engaged. The teacher will then take action to respond to this and usually stop the activity to speak to the whole class to clarify what is expected of them. Another example is when the teacher provides additional support during an activity for learners when they come across a problem. A further example is when the teacher intervenes with a learner that is making good progress to provide additional challenge using higher-order questioning. These opportunities for Assessment for Learning are not formal and may not make it to the lesson plan, but they are necessary for learning to be at its best.

Assessment for Learning is at its most effective when it is **formative,** i.e. when learners respond to the information that they are being given in order to improve their performance. Using the example above, this would be when learners respond to the clarification regarding the task and are able to undertake this and, therefore, to achieve the learning objective. Responses to more formal Assessment for Learning opportunities can be even more effective, such as in response to written feedback. In recent years, some schools have used whole-school strategies to enable learners to engage with feedback by integrating it into lessons. Examples of these include "the purple pen of progress," where teachers write their feedback and then learners use a purple pen to write their response to the feedback. Another version is D.I.R.T. – directed, independent, reflection time. While it is important to adhere to school-wide policies, it is more important to understand the principles underpinning such practice to ensure that it has the impact required. This then allows the teacher to consider how to implement the strategies for maximum effect on learner progress, rather than just go through the motions.

Reflection point:

Consider a class that you have observed or have taught:

1 What are your expectations for these learners?
2 What do you know about their skills and capabilities?
3 What do you expect them to achieve at the end of a lesson, by the end of the topic, or by the end of the qualification?
4 At what points do you, or the class teacher, respond to what learners know or don't know?
5 When is the assessment at its most formative? How do you know?

Learning theory

It can be easy to assume that learning theory is abstract from good practice in the classroom. However, learning theory provides us with insights into how learners learn, and how we choose to teach. It can challenge our own assumptions and mental models of what teaching is based on our previous experiences. In Chapter 6 "Learning and Teaching Strategies: Differentiation," we will take a closer look at learning theory. Here we investigate how learning theory impacts on the approaches that are taken regarding Assessment for Learning and how it is implemented in the classroom. In particular, we will focus on the place of Behaviourism and Constructivism.

Behaviourism takes the approach that we can influence the learning behaviour of learners by the approach that we take to their learning. For example, by setting a clear task and rewarding the successful completion of that task learners will learn what the "right" answer is and reproduce this in the future. The teacher will then set a subsequent task that is more difficult than the original task, and by using the same sort of reward structure as previously will result in learning. This approach assumes that **learning is linear** and will be learned in carefully scaffolded steps, going from simple to more difficult concepts. The consequences of this approach to learning are frequently seen in classrooms. Learning objectives are clearly stated at the start of the lesson, the success criteria is carefully explained to learners, and learners are then assessed against those criteria, with feedback focusing on the extent to which the success criteria have been achieved. Many schools and classrooms use the format of "What went well; Even better if" in order to structure feedback in a way that learners will understand and respond to.

There are significant benefits to this approach: learners can be seen having confidence in their learning and understanding exactly what is required of them. At both Level 2 and Level 3, it can allow learners to have a good understanding of their subject and qualification assessment requirements, but it can be argued that this approach limits learning. Moreover, it can be seen to address the key principles of effective Assessment for Learning (AfL) as identified by the Assessment Reform Group. However, there can be the temptation that by using this approach learners will be "taught to the test" and this approach will not challenge the most able learners, nor allow the class to benefit from the range of insight that will exist within the classroom.

Constructivism takes a different approach to the learning behaviour of learners. Under the constructivist theory to learning, knowledge and understanding are co-developed between learners and the teacher. The constructivist theory recognises that the teacher needs to identify what learners already know and to be able to use the expertise within the class to develop everybody's knowledge and understanding. The intention is to teach within Lev Vygotsky's "zone of proximal development (ZPD)," i.e., to scaffold learning skillfully so that each learner knows, understands, and can do more at the end of the lesson than when he/she came into the room. By using this approach, greater levels of differentiation can be planned for and include greater levels of stretch and challenge for the most able learners. To implement this approach, learners need to be provided with alternative tasks and questioning needs to be more open ended than would be the case with a more behaviourist approach.

Under the constructivist approach, learning is considered to be **an interactive process**, including both the learners and the teacher, where assessment is identifying what learners know, understand, and can do to develop further learning, i.e., to be formative. The process of assessment gains its own purpose in teaching, which is to constantly improve rather than the achievement of grades (or learning objectives). For the most able in the class who may find that the achievement of the top grades of the qualification relatively easy, this approach can be used to challenge them to do more. In some instances, this will mean working at a level above the qualification that is being taught. If this is the case, then this approach may mean that learners may be better prepared for the next stage of their education. In other instances, it may mean allowing learners to think more widely than the qualification requires and, thereby, encourage an enthusiasm for the subject of Business (or Economics or Enterprise, etc.) and a more in-depth understanding of the business world and wider economy. In other instances, being involved in national business competitions or engaging in finding solutions to local business problems can enable learners to develop a range of transferable skills that will support them in later life. Alternatively, this can just be fun and engage learners more fully in their learning.

As can be seen, both Behaviourism and Constructivism have their benefits and should not be seen as being in competition with each other or mutually exclusive. Rather it should provide you as the teacher with greater breadth in the range of approaches you use to enable your learners to be successful and to enjoy their learning.

Reflection point:

Consider your own experiences of teaching Business and/or Economics.

1 When were you most inspired by the subject?
2 When did you know that you were doing well with the subject?
3 When did you feel at your most confident?
4 In each of those situations, how did the approaches to assessment vary and how aware were you of being assessed?

Sharing objectives and working with success criteria

So far, we have looked at what Assessment for Learning is, what it seeks to do, and different approaches that will enable you to build an Assessment for Learning (AfL) repertoire. From this point we will begin to look at specific strategies and ways of implementing AfL. As has already been stated, understanding what your learners know about a subject and the range of skills that they have in relation to a topic is only the starting point. It is then up to the teacher to enable learners to develop from that point. In terms of planning, this usually comes from setting the learning objectives for that lesson. Identifying whether or not each learner is able to achieve the learning objectives will be through the assessment of achievement against those learning objectives. In the lesson plan extract, next to each learning objective is a description of how the learning objective will be assessed by the teacher. This is only successful when there is **constructive alignment** or **assessment validity**, i.e. where what is being assessed matches the learning objective.

Have a look at this section from a lesson plan on Enterprise Education:

Learning objectives	*Assessment strategy*
Learning Objective 1: Identify a range of enterprise skills.	Targeted questioning during starter activity. Learners will mark each other's work against the list of enterprise skills that are provided on the PowerPoint (peer assessment). Learners will receive their scores back from each other straight after the activity.
Learning Objective 2: Develop team working skills.	(*Presentation task*) Teacher questioning and peer assessment through peer assessment sheets. Peer assessment sheets will be given to each learner. Learners will then assess the other groups against the criteria of: • logo of the chocolate bar and quality of explanation • selling price of the chocolate bar and quality of justification The combination of these two will determine the winner of the task.

If we look at the table above, we can see that Learning Objective 1 is about identifying a range of enterprise skills, which are to be assessed against a list provided by the teacher. If these two elements are seen to match each other, then they are aligned.

Learning Objective 2 is about developing team working skills. Here the assessment strategy is based on the quality of the explanation and the justification of ideas within a presentation. While it could be argued that the quality of the presentation is due to effective teamworking, this is not a foregone conclusion. It could easily be the case that one member dominated the group, did all the work, and then produced the presentation. In this case, the quality of the presentation will reflect the ability of the dominant team member, and therefore, there is no alignment between the objective and the assessment.

As Learning Objective 2 is to develop team working skills, then there would need to be an assessment of individual skills at the start of the activity and at the end of the activity. There should be clear identification of what makes for good team working skills.

The choice of lesson has been deliberate so that it is not specifically linked to a qualification or level. Chapter 5 "Learning and Teaching Strategies: working with assessment criteria" is written to address the specific assessment requirements of academic and vocational qualifications, and it will provide examples of how learning objectives and assessments will be appropriate to identify and develop learner learning within them. This also builds on the examples provided in Chapter 2 "Getting Started: Teaching Academic Subjects" and Chapter 3 "Getting Started: Teaching Vocational Subjects," and the ways in which starters and lesson objectives can be used to engage learners and assess their levels of knowledge and understanding. The text below will address the underlying principles of good teaching and learning to support learner success, whether that is in a lesson designed to develop learner exam skills or for those lessons that are for broader educational experience.

Sharing learning intentions or objectives with learners is important for motivating and engaging learners, as well as providing opportunities for the teacher to assess and respond to the quality of the learning of their learners. Recognising that the intentions or objectives have a role in motivating learners will have an impact on how these are shared with learners. If doing so is seen as a way of settling the class, then reading them out and getting learners to write them in their books may suffice. However, if they are to be used to really engage learners in their own learning, then a range of strategies will be used, for example:

- Discussing them with the class.
- Using questions to link previous learning to this lesson's learning.
- Providing a thought-provoking starter linked to the theme of the lesson.
- Getting learners to develop their own success criteria.
- Taking out the verbs in the learning objectives.
- Getting learners to identify the most appropriate level from Bloom's taxonomy.

All of these would be designed to provide learners with some ownership of their learning, rather than being passive recipients of what they are being told.

Alongside the sharing of the learning objectives is the need for learners to **understand the success criteria,** i.e. how do they know that they have achieved the learning objective to a sufficient quality or high-enough standard. Moreover, is there a way of enabling learners to take ownership of the success criteria to empower them in their own learning? In many instances, this will be linked to the assessment objectives of a qualification. Where this is the case, the learning objectives will be phrased using *trigger words and phrases* from exams and the success criteria will come from *the qualification mark schemes*. Enabling learners to self-assess and peer assess the answers to exam questions is one way that they can come to grips with the success criteria and learn to provide answers that maximise their marks.

However, if your approach to teaching is to be wholly focused on exam skills, then motivation will suffer (yours and the learners') and learners will see education in very mechanistic terms. Identifying a wide range of skills and capabilities that you want to develop at the start of the course and introducing them into your lessons with specific success criteria will provide a much richer experience for learners. This can include skills such as: presentation, negotiation, communication, and financial literacy. In addition, certain skills, such as analysis and evaluation, are important for life but rarely need to be undertaken in exam conditions and in exam-style answers. Enabling learners to use these skills in different contexts is also important. To give full value to developing these skills in these lessons learners will also need to understand the success criteria associated with these skills and to be able to self-assess and peer-assess in order to empower themselves in their own learning. This will be addressed further in Chapter 7 "Developing wider skills: seeing beyond the specification."

"In Lesson" Assessment for Learning approaches and strategies

There is an almost infinite range of strategies that are available to download from various websites and I recommend that you use these to introduce variety into your lessons. This section is intended to make links between the various strategies that you could use within your lessons and their purpose.

In many texts on Assessment for Learning the place of learner engagement/enjoyment is missed. Yet almost every teacher knows that getting learners involved in their own learning is beneficial to them as well as to the teacher. Using social media, or examples from the media, are helpful methods for this. The following approaches are ones that are in use at the moment - Snapchat and WhatsApp style messages – whereby a learner writes a short message, in the style that he/she would for Snapchat or WhatsApp on what he/she has learnt in the class to someone who has missed the lesson. This works well as a plenary to the lesson. Another strategy taken from the media is the mannequin challenge, where learners could work in a group to "model" what had been covered in the previous class lesson. The student who missed the lesson has to work out what had been done in class. Crime Scene Investigation programmes are popular TV shows; this approach can be used for end-of-module "tests." Instead of a traditional written response to a case study, the classroom can be set up as a crime scene with clues that learners have to unpick in order to analyse the business problem, e.g. why the owner absconded leaving debts in their wake can be effectively linked to cashflow statement analysis.

Teacher assessment continues to be the main form of assessment, for both formative and summative purposes, Formative assessment is when there is a clear intention to improve learners' skills and understanding. For this to happen learners need to be able to respond and improve. This can be very simple, such as through discussion in the classroom where the teacher uses the answer to a question to identify whether further clarification is needed to address a misconception, or whether more difficult questions will allow learners to extend their understanding. The use of a quizzes - such as the game-based format of Kahoot! - have become popular and can be used very effectively for formative purposes, where the teacher responds quickly to any misconceptions identified in learner responses.

Another simple approach is that of "traffic lights," where learners use red, amber or green objects to identify their level of understanding. The traffic lights can be suitably coloured cups or laminated squares. The learner will show when they understand (green), don't understand (red), or are not sure (amber). An effective teacher will respond to those learners whose traffic light is red either individually or by bringing them together and addressing their difficulty as a group.

Written feedback to written answers continues to be a significant aspect of the teacher's role - but it is only formative if learners have an opportunity to improve their response either to the same question or to a similar question. A straightforward example is the regular use of case study questions as homework. This will work best if:

a   There is constructive feedback provided in order to improve case study writing skills.

b   The nature of the feedback links very clearly to the mark scheme for the case study.

c   The written feedback is supported by a review of the case study in the subsequent lesson, which allows learners to clarify their understanding of what makes a good response.

d   There is the opportunity for learners to undertake a further case study within a short timeframe to implement their improved understanding of what is required.

What is important to remember is that good formative assessment takes time and must be allowed for when planning both schemes of work and individual lessons.

Another form of teacher assessment is that of summative assessment or assessment of learning, which is commonly used within lessons. In addition to the end of module test, there are situations where individual learning objectives are assessed *within* the lesson. An example of this is the visual approach of identifying the assessment point with a "pit stop" or a "bus stop." In this assessment, when a learning objective has been covered a picture of a "pit stop" or a "bus stop" appears on the screen, which provides a visual reminder to learners that their learning of that objective is about to be tested, perhaps with "traffic lights" or with "thumbs up, thumbs down." While a number of teachers will say that this is assessment *for* learning, if there is no significant checking of understanding and difficulties are not addressed then it is only assessment *of* learning. This is not to devalue what is being undertaken, as it can add pace to a lesson and develop learners' confidence in their skills.

The alternative to teacher assessment is learner assessment, either of themselves (self-assessment) or of another learner (peer assessment). The purpose of this is to develop learner understanding and skill with regards to the relevant assessment criteria, and it can be used in both coursework and non-coursework lessons. As already indicated, for this to be effective there will need to be careful planning within schemes of work and lesson plans so that learners become confident in their ability to assess and to provide appropriate feedback.

How this works is that where learners are working on the same task, at an appropriate point in the lesson, the teacher can ask learners to change desks or swap work and read the work of their peers using the assessment criteria to identify what has been achieved and to what standard. This can be homework, coursework, or other activities that are undertaken within a lesson. Using a Post-it® note or a different coloured pen, learners provide feedback against the assessment criteria. Learners (either by themselves or with a peer) are then given the opportunity to improve the quality of their work.

There is a note of caution with learners using self-feedback and peer feedback when learners are developing skills. The teacher still needs to assess the work and the feedback on a regular basis. When learners have acquired the necessary skills, the teacher still needs to standardise regularly.

This section has made connections between strategies that are used in the classroom and the purposes of assessment *for* learning. This section also highlighted the fact that what is sometimes called assessment *for* learning is actually assessment *of* learning. The end of this section provides you with an opportunity to reflect on your own practice. The next section will identify where teacher assessment is less productive than self-assessment or peer assessment.

Reflection point:

1 In your own scheme of work, when do you include opportunities for learners to respond to feedback?
2 What approaches does your school use?
3 What would you like to introduce?
4 Do you think your learners are getting better at answering questions or are they plateauing?
5 Do you need to try an alternative approach?

Assessment of enterprise and/or work-related learning

Ofsted, enterprise coordinators, and formal research all recognise that assessment of enterprise skills and enterprise events are challenging and usually lack strategic oversight. In the current educational context, Enterprise and employability has been conflated as is clearly seen in the Ofsted (2016) report, *Getting Ready for Work*, which investigated the availability and effectiveness of Enterprise Education and work-related learning for learners in secondary schools. While the report, as well as other reports, into Enterprise Education/work-related learning may question our understanding and expectations of the role of education, the more pragmatic question for this chapter is how to assess Enterprise Education. As the Ofsted (2016) report makes clear, schools often fail to formally assess learning in this area or make the most of opportunities to have learning accredited, reflecting the lack of value that most senior leadership teams ascribe to Enterprise Education.

As with any block of learning, the starting point is to identify the knowledge and skills that learners need to develop (i.e. learning aims and objectives). While the list of Enterprise knowledge and skills is quite fluid, it generally includes teamwork, communication, risk taking, creativity, and problem solving. Within the Key Stage 4 National Mathematics Curriculum is the requirement for learners to be able to apply their mathematical skills within financial contexts. As the teacher, you may have considerable control over the identification of Enterprise skills that you want to develop and you can make this specific to the group.

Having decided what skills and knowledge are to be developed, then the level of skill and knowledge should be age appropriate. It shouldn't be the case that a 17-year-old learner provides the same answer as a 12-year-old learner to the question of "What makes for good teamwork?" Although my observations would imply that this is often acceptable. For example, it would be appropriate for a Year 12 or Year 13 learner to be able to identify his/her role within a team using an assessment tool, such as Meredith Belbin's Team Roles, and use this to evaluate the effectiveness of the team. For a Year 7 learner, a simpler set of expectations would be used, such as being able to identify that he/she is helpful to others on the team and to give examples of this.

As the purpose of the event is to enable learners to improve their knowledge and skills, the assessment needs to take place at the start of the event as well as at the end of the event, showing progress. Where there is a strategic and whole-year implementation of Enterprise Education, then the opportunities for assessment will need to reflect this. In some schools, the idea of an Enterprise Passport has been used so that they can record their use and development of Enterprise skills throughout the year.

Continuing with the theme of teamwork, learners could be given a set of success criteria that enable them to either self-assess or peer assess their skills at both the start and end of the event. The reason for using self-assessment or peer assessment is two-fold. One is that it encourages independent learning and self-regulation, which are both important work-related and Enterprise skills, although ones that you may be reluctant to assess. Secondly, enterprise events are often implemented as a large-group event. Consequently, it is very difficult to implement effective teacher assessment for every learner.

In conclusion to this section, Enterprise Education (and work-related learning) should be treated as any other aspect of learning - with clear objectives and success criteria together with assessment against those success criteria. The main difference is that self-assessment and peer assessment has a much more significant role due to the limitations placed upon teachers when assessing large numbers at a single point in time.

Reflection point:

Consider an Enterprise Education event that you have been a part of:

1 What were the objectives of the event?
2 How did you know if you were successful?
3 Were those skills transferable? How do you know?

Challenges – and how to manage them

The constantly increasing demands on school accountability by Government, the Secretary of State for Education, and Ofsted has meant that schools and colleges are scrutinised for the quality of learning. This began with the introduction of School League Tables in 1992 and is currently focused on Progress 8. With Progress 8, the progress of all learners from year 7 to year 11 within a high school is assessed against eight key subjects for GCSE or Level 2. Not only this, but the progress of different groups is tracked and compared against other groups, both within the school and against national benchmark data e.g.

- Male achievement against female achievement (within the school and then each against national data).
- Disadvantaged against non-disadvantaged (within the school and against national benchmark data).
- Those with English as an Additional Language (EAL) against those whose first language is English.

As a consequence of this, schools have constantly increased the amount of information that they hold and also the amount of assessment and tracking that is being undertaken, without necessarily evaluating the effectiveness of the approaches that they are taking. For the teacher, this has become a question of **manageability,** with an apparently never-ending increase in assessment workload.

Within this there are specific challenges for the teacher. While an individual teacher or department will always have to work following the school policies and procedures, there can be ways in which a teacher can respond to these challenges. Three challenges that contribute to the issue of manageability are raised and addressed below.

Challenge 1: **Data overload**, *with the result that the child/young person becomes a data set and not a person.*

The first response is to remember that learners are children and not data sets. Data sets tend to identify expected grades based on national benchmarking, which can be useful. However, research consistently shows the most significant influence on learners' learning is the teacher's expectations of them together with the quality of the teacher's relationship with learners, i.e. if you believe and expect learners to achieve highly (and act accordingly) then your learners will go on to achieve highly. My favourite example of this was observing a Year 10 BTEC Level 2 Business class within a school operating within a socially deprived area. The majority of the class were white boys; white boys from low socioeconomic backgrounds are identified nationally as the lowest performing group and the hardest to reach. The case study and source materials were from *The Guardian* newspaper. While there was some strategic input by the teacher in terms of key terms and vocabulary for the article, learners engaged with this fully and produced some very good data analysis at a level that some A level classes would struggle with. Inevitably, these learners went on to achieve significantly higher than the national benchmark data would have predicted.

Challenge 2: *The assessment is used to* **track and monitor learner performance** *rather than use assessment to respond to their learning, i.e. there is an increase in summative assessment rather than a genuine formative assessment.*

Tracking of learner progress should not be an end in and of itself. Working with learners and enabling them to engage with their own progress is a powerful tool, which can be managed in a number of different ways, for example, individual tutorials or colour-coded assessment grids showing when they are working above, at, and below target. In addition, these trackers can be used to identify not only those topics that learners struggle with but also key skills. Therefore, teachers have to be able to assess strategically, which is a way of ensuring manageability of the assessment load.

The volume of assessment is something that affects - or afflicts - both learners and the teacher. This is true of both in-class and out-of-class assessment. Looking first at in-class assessment - not every learning objective will need to be assessed by writing in a booklet and then recorded at the end of the lesson. Sometimes a show of hands will be sufficient. Deciding where your efforts, and those of your learners, should be will influence the type of assessment you carry out. In terms of enabling your learners to achieve maximum marks on exams, you will want to spend the time on writing longer answers, which will require an investment in assessment terms. In contrast, definitions can be assessed using a quick Kahoot! quiz.

The volume of assessment also affects homework. There are still teachers that set homework without really considering what it is that they want to assess. Using a simple example, the teacher sets 20 questions for the same outcome: Can your learners calculate the acid test ratio? The teacher will know after five questions if learners can do this. Either they can calculate the ratio, or they will have got it wrong 20 times and become thoroughly demoralised. Being very specific about what you want your learners to learn will mean that you reduce the amount of homework you set, and therefore mark, and spend longer on meaningful reviews of learning within the classroom. Therefore, rather than asking your learners to calculate the acid test ratio 20 times, it may be more meaningful to provide different results linked to one or two specific business scenarios and ask them to analyse the health of the business in light of this. This could then be used to develop discussions in class enabling learners to develop analytical and evaluative skills. After an in-class informative discussion, a writing task could follow whereby learners have to display their written analytical and evaluative skills. This task could then be peer assessed, improving their ownership and understanding of assessment and reducing the teacher workload. While assessment and assessment for learning will always be a challenge, keeping focused on what is important will enable learners to achieve more and to be engaged and invested in their learning.

Challenge 3: *Schools introduce* **procedures for assessment rather than processes**. *For example, a school introduces the practice of using "the purple pen of progress" so that every piece of feedback that learners have to respond to contains writing in purple pen to show that they have done this.*

The underlying principle is that learners need to engage with feedback in order to improve their learning. The procedure for this is relatively unimportant. More significant is the process that learners engage with. As above in the discussions where formative assessment/learning was taking place, the written work would be the evidence of learning. Peer assessment could then be used to allow for further development, and the school procedure could be used. But it is much more important for learners to participate in their learning.

Linking Assessment for Learning (AfL) to differentiation

While **differentiation** and **Assessment for Learning** are often described as separate entities, as indicated by the fact that we have separate chapters on these subjects, the reality is that they are two sides of the same coin and should work in tandem. In practice, what this means is that when the teacher undertakes effective assessment during a lesson, then it should have an impact on the differentiation that is undertaken during the next lesson. This is above and beyond the differentiation that will take place in order to take into account other needs, such as Special Education Needs and Disability (SEND) and English as an Additional Language (EAL).

An example of this is during a lesson on cashflow forecasting. At the end of the lesson, all learners had made good progress. Some learners had completed the main activity, which was to complete a cashflow forecast using information from a case study. Not only had they completed this, but through individual Question & Answer (Q&A) it had been ascertained that they understood what the process was and could undertake some simple analysis of the data. This group of learners is now ready to move ahead onto more difficult analysis.

Another group of learners have not yet completed the cashflow forecast. Through individual Q&A, it is clear that they understand what they are doing and will be able to complete this at the start of the next lesson. There is one learner who is completing the cashflow forecast but doesn't understand what she is doing. This end-of-lesson assessment will inform the planning for the next lesson so that all learners are able to move on from where they are and continue to make good progress.

For this to happen, the teacher will need to *differentiate* the following lesson. This may mean using a simple review activity at the start of the next lesson and then provide more challenging analysis questions for those who have completed and understand what they are doing, and provide time for the second group to complete the cashflow forecast and some simple analytical questions. The individual who is struggling can gain additional support from the teacher while the others are continuing with their work. After a suitable period, the teacher will review what has been accomplished as a whole-class activity, where learners self-assess and add to their notes from the work that the others have completed. This brings the class to the same point of being able to complete the cashflow forecast and analyse the data.

Conclusion

Assessment and Assessment for Learning (AfL), is a significant part of being a successful teacher and is an area that much has been written about. Within this chapter, we have looked at different aspects of assessment in generic terms. In the next chapter, we will look at specific assessment objectives of different types of qualifications and how to ensure that learners are able to work with the assessment objectives and develop the requisite key skills.

References

Assessment Reform Group (2002). Assessment for Learning: 10 principles Research-based principles to guide classroom practice (online). Available from: https://www.aaia.org.uk/content/uploads/2010/06/Assessment-for-Learning-10-principles.pdf [Accessed 21 January 2019]

Belbin, R. Meredith (2010). *Team Roles at Work*. London, New York: Routledge.

Black, Paul and Wiliam, Dylan (1998). *Inside the Black Box: Raising Standards Through Classroom Assessment*. London: King's College Lond.

Department for Children, Schools and Families (2008). *The Assessment for Learning Strategy*, Nottingham: DCSF Publications.

Department for Education (2014). Mathematics programmes of study: key stage 4 National curriculum in England. Crown Copyright No. DFE-00496-2014 (online). Available from: https://assets.publishing.service.gov.uk/government/uploads/system/uploads/attachment_data/file/331882/KS4_maths_PoS_FINAL_170714.pdf [Accessed 21 January 2019] Ref:

Kahoot! (online). Available from: https://kahoot.com/ [Accessed 21 January 2019]

Ofsted (2016). *Getting Ready for Work*. Manchester: Crown Copyright No. 160056.

5

LEARNING AND TEACHING STRATEGIES

Working with assessment criteria

- • An introduction to working with assessment criteria
- • Meeting exam board criteria
- • What will be asked in the exam?
- • Assessment objectives
- • Meeting assessment objectives through activities in the classroom
- • Bloom's taxonomy
- • Resources
- • Regular assessment
- • Conclusion

An introduction to working with assessment criteria

Early in my teaching career I was asked to review the work of a teacher in another part of the country as his learners consistently underperformed in their A level exams. This was done by reviewing a set of learner answers taken from a mock exam. It was transparent that while learners understood the subject they did not know how to respond to the questions set in a way that enabled them to achieve highly. It was a significant lesson in the importance of working with the exam criteria and the impact that failing to do so both on learners and on the teacher.

The word *assessment* is almost a mantra in most schools and colleges, regardless of the subject that is taught. Today, it is *the* single criteria through which academic progress is measured and not only impacts on learners' progress in their academic career but can also affect the reputation of the teacher and the school. Knowing this, this mantra can send shivers down the spines of trainees and newly qualified teachers. Team it with the word *criteria* and it can often be enough to send some trainees into a state of self-doubt and panic about what assessment criteria actually is, how to implement it into lessons, and whether the standards of assessment that are being used are correct.

Working with the specification assessment criteria can provide teachers with the boundaries that ensure learners are rewarded appropriately for the level of knowledge the learners have demonstrated with the appropriate level of skill. By working with these criteria in a regular manner, teachers are informed that learners are making progress and striving towards the standards that are at the right level for their individual progress. Determining the "right level of individual progress" is usually done by using previous student performance data compared to national benchmarking data and results in the provision of "target grades." Learners are then deemed to be making the "right level of individual progress" when they are working at a level that will enable them to meet their expected target grade. There is a lot of debate concerning the use of target grades: some learners' target grades are too inflated, some learners make far more progress in ways that is not recognised or rewarded, or the learner simply coasts because the target grade is not challenging enough.

The target grade is set to evidence "value added" in learner progress and to measure the success of the overall course. By benchmarking against a national measure, the success and achievement of the course can be compared to other like-for-like courses throughout the country. Furthermore, and more importantly, it provides regulatory bodies such as Ofsted (the Office for Standards in Education, Children's Services and Skill) with an insight – although somewhat limited – of the quality of provision offered to learners. This explains why educational establishments place such importance on the role of assessment in the teaching and learning cycle. Having said all this, without assessment – whether it is formal, informal, formative, or summative – it is difficult to gauge whether learners have grasped what they have spent time learning in the classroom, and whether or not they are actually making progress.

What this means for us as teachers is that we have to make sure to include sufficient assessment in our lessons, throughout the duration of the course, to ensure that at any given point of the course we are aware of the learning and progress that is taking place. We also have to make certain that this learning is at the correct level, allowing learners to meet the knowledge and skill level as suggested by the exam board. This monitoring of progress against specification criteria will allow you to ensure that you consistently assess against the appropriate and relevant standards and can realistically track learner progress. Where necessary, concerns with regards to academic progress can be highlighted at the earliest opportunity, and measures can be put in place to support learners to achieve their target grade.

To ensure that assessment is completed in a rigorous and consistent way, schools and colleges will timetable formal and informal assessment dates into the school calendar. This allows teachers, learners, and parents to be aware of when the assessment will take place and the type of assessment it is. Some teachers also find this quite helpful as they can begin to think about interleaving and selecting the appropriate topics for assessment. This is done by familiarising themselves with the assessment objectives and mark schemes so that the appropriate feedback can be offered *and* acted upon for progress. This is important as during feedback the language used should be reflective of what the assessment criteria states in each of the boundaries. This allows learners to become familiar with the criteria and how they can be met in terms of quality of knowledge and detail. Annotation of the learners' responses by highlighting/identifying where each assessment objective has been met is one of the best ways of doing this. This allows learners to see what they are doing right. This further allows learners (and their parents) to have a clearer insight of the level of progress that has been made, and what needs to be done to make further improvements and progress.

Accuracy in assessment is a skill that may take a while to acquire. However, in order to allow learners to succeed, not only do you need to know how to assess the grades, but you also need to be able to instill knowledge and strategies in your learners that will allow them to achieve good grades. As well as sharing good learner responses with the rest of the group, guiding learners towards recognising this skill for themselves also helps them make effective progress. "Live marking" is a great way of escalating learner progress; this is where one learner's work is placed on the board, and either the teacher or the other learners in the class assess the work against the suggested criteria. Familiarising yourself with the criteria and the mark scheme is essential in ensuring that learners gain maximum benefit from this activity as you guide the learners correctly towards what should and should not be included.

Another valuable strategy is **modelling**. This is where you write a response to a question explaining and modelling what to include in an assessment question so that learners can achieve maximum marks. Modelling is a good strategy to adopt when learners are first introduced to exam-style assessment questions so that they have good grounding of how to attempt them. It is equally important when learners are attempting to master skills for the more highly valued questions requiring analysis and evaluation skills.

Consequently, awareness of exam criteria and how to meet them is extremely important and will require an investment of your time and resources. On the whole, **live marking and modelling**, where learners are *actually* able to see what could be included in a response to an exam question and how to achieve the marks are the best methods through which learners feel that they can confidently demonstrate their own skills. Once they have seen a well-written response, and understood how the marks were achieved, learners are more likely to produce a more confident response. This does not mean that you have to do all the modelling and live marking yourself. You can ask other learners to live mark or model their work, which is a great way of engaging learners and ensuring that they really do know what the demands of the question are and how to meet them.

Reflection point: Consider your own experiences of preparing for public exams, such as GCSEs or A levels.

1 What were the methods that your teachers used to prepare you for the exams?
2 Which were successful? Why?

Meeting exam board criteria

The best place to start is to carry out research such as analysing past paper questions, their mark schemes as well as the examiner's report. The **mark scheme** will provide you with insight into the content and level of detail required for each of the questions. The **examiner's report** will take this further, as responses received in each individual question are scrutinised and discuss exactly what the examiner was looking for, as well as what the shortcomings of those who did not provide the correct responses. This level of research will allow you to familiarise yourself with the language that is used in exam papers, key phrases used in questioning, and key terms that examiners are looking for in learner responses and mark allocation. The benefit of this is that it will allow you to tailor individual activities in your lessons towards the varying levels of assessment criteria, which form the basis of the demands of the

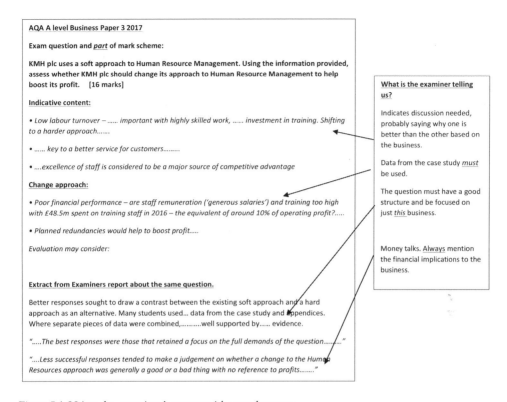

Figure 5.1 Using the examiner's report with your learners.

question and guide your learners towards gaining confidence in accurately respond-ing to exam-style questions. Sharing small, relevant extracts of the examiner's report with learners through which they are able to see for themselves what the examiner has said can be extremely effective, as it adds credence to what you would like to instill in them (see Figure 5.1). Even at GCSE level, learners are interested in, and have the ability to understand what the examiner is reporting. However, for this to be effective, it has to be structured appropriately. This means that it has to be broken down into bite-sized chunks for learners to be able to digest. In addition, you must fully understand what the examiner is saying prior to sharing it with your learners, so that you can offer further explanation should your learners need it.

What will be asked in the exam?

This is often the basis of conversations amongst trainee teachers and teachers, between trainee teachers and mentors, and more importantly, between teachers and learners. With regards to assessment criteria, queries on the whole, are based on the type and style of questioning that the exam board will be using to check the skill and knowledge learners have acquired over the duration of the course. Similarly, learners and their par-ents not only want to know about the type and style of questioning they should expect on the exam paper, but what the teacher is going to do to effectively prepare learners for success in the exam and in meeting their target grades. In essence, how can learners meet the assessment criteria? Trainee teachers will often ask similar questions. How can they effectively prepare their learners for the exam? When asked these questions, mentors often respond with: "The exam board can ask anything, so to get a good grade, respond by using similar language as that used in model answers provided by the exam board." Although this is good sound advice, the best way to prepare your learners is to make them aware of what forms of assessment there are and inform them, both learners and parents, that assessment will take place regularly during the course through different formats in order to test their knowledge and skills in various ways.

Assessment objectives

Assessment criteria is made up of several levels, often categorised under the heading of assessment objectives (AOs). For most exam boards this means that learners have to meet 4 levels: For both Eduqas and AQA exam boards [both accessed 21 January 2019] they are:

Assessment objective	Requirements from learner	Command words used in the question
AO1	Demonstrate knowledge and understanding	State, name, list, identify, define
AO2	Apply knowledge and understanding	Apply, use, explain, calculate, illustrate, show, adapt, interpret
AO3	Analyse/analysis of the issues	Analyse, compare and contrast, explain, distinguish, examine
AO4	Evaluate the information to make informed judgements.	Discuss, argue, recommend, advise, justify, consider, to what extent, assess

This really is the crux of the assessment criteria: Each assessment objective will be worth a certain percentage of the final mark. This information is available on the exam board websites. Examiners will include a variety of questions and questioning techniques in the exam so that the individual assessment objectives can be met by learners through which they can achieve the dedicated marks in the given category. For learners, this means that not only do they have to demonstrate the correct level of knowledge, they also have to demonstrate the correct level of skill in transmitting that knowledge to the examiner. The adeptness with which they can do this is dependent on the amount of practice that they have had in attempting questions of that calibre under timed conditions, received feedback for improvement, and acted on that feedback to improve their responses and received feedback, once again on the level of progress. This highlights the impact of a well-thought-through assessment process.

As mentioned in Chapter 2 "Getting Started: Teaching Academic Subjects," without ample opportunity to practice, learners are more likely to panic under pressure and not fully answer the questions through which they can achieve the marks they deserve, and which will allow them to achieve their target grade. Time constraints can place much pressure on learners, causing them to provide incorrect responses to the questions. This makes the time in the classroom extremely valuable in working with assessment criteria. This is the place where learners have access to their teacher, their peers and other resources such as books, mark schemes and examiner reports. Through these the learners can begin to learn and master their skills which will allow them to meet the assessment criteria.

Achieving skills in assessment is a step-by-step process and can take the better part of a two-year course. This incremental approach is essential in ensuring that learners are able to see the value of assessment and the role it plays in their learning instead of becoming completely overwhelmed by it. Furthermore, links need to be made with earlier knowledge through interleaving for holistic learning. These are tested using both formative and summative styles of assessment. Assessments are not necessarily a negative aspect of teaching and learning. They can be a motivational tool for learners as they can see their progress and gain confidence in what they are capable of achieving, especially if they are keeping track of their marks. Therefore, an individual progress tracker that helps learners keep a track of their own marks can be a useful tool to do this. It can allow learners to see the relevance of assessment and give them more time to prepare for these.

The benefit of assessing in line with assessment criteria is that you work with a rigorous set of standards that ensure consistency and impartiality. Through this set of standards, you are able to assess the success of your teaching and learning strategies and activities. The argument is that the accuracy of learner responses is reflective of teacher input. Any patterns of poor understanding can be highlighted as material that needs re-visiting, or re-teaching, so that learners' knowledge can be corrected. This indicator is absolutely essential in ensuring that learners are armed with the best possible skills, advice, and knowledge through which they can achieve the assessment objectives.

Meeting assessment objectives through activities in the classroom

Assessment plays a key role in the lesson. Once learners have the knowledge, assessment informs us of how well the information has been acquired and understood. Assessment is also used from lesson to lesson to ensure how much knowledge has been retained and to what standard that knowledge has been retained. Learners can be assessed from the moment that they step into the classroom; multiple choice, mix-and-match, or quick two- and four-mark questions are great at this part of this lesson. Not only do we want the activity to be snappy, we want it to be interesting so that it will channel learners thinking towards *this* lesson and disconnect from the lesson before. Aware that they will be assessed, albeit, informally, will force learners to re-cap their notes, which will make the activity more engaging and contribute to learners remembering the knowledge, even though it may just be basic. Starter activities are generally used to either:

a   To remind learners of what was learnt in previous lessons.

 or

b   To gauge what learners may already be aware of or can deduce from our hints about a new topic that we are about to teach.

As the aim of the starter activity is to take up less than 10 minutes, it provides a rapid assessment of learner knowledge. The assessment criteria that is generally being sought to be met at this stage of the lesson is usually of a low level, which is reflective of the skills and knowledge that they will be asked to display for Assessment Objectives 1 or 2. Questions generally ask learners to recall, define, describe, explain, find contrasting examples of, or even in brief, provide a solution.

Activities that require learners to do this include:

- General quizzes
- Multiple-choice questions
- In less than 20 words (e.g. Tell me what you know about fiscal policy.)
- 3 of 3 (e.g. Answer 3 questions on 3 different topics.)
- In 3 mins – To a given scenario, provide an advantage (something positive), a disadvantage (something negative), and a best course of action (something that is best to do). (e.g. "A local business is growing rapidly. Discuss options of international growth with the owner.")
- Beat the clock (e.g. Answer as many questions as possible in less than a minute on monetary and fiscal policy.)

As well as the example of activities above, another good learning strategy is to provide learners with the opportunity to peer assess each other's work. With guidance, learners can do this efficiently and identify whether or not the person whose work they are marking has met the assessment criteria or not. In doing this, learners can improve their own responses too. Further, a deeper level of learning can take place by asking learners to explain the marks they have awarded, why they have awarded the marks, and how learners can improve their work.

Bloom's taxonomy

To keep the momentum of the lesson, and keep learners sufficiently challenged, learners may be asked to:

- Examine a particular business, and in relation to the problem, consider and **suggest** all the options available to them.
- Explain the **benefits and drawbacks** to the business of each of the available options.
- **Recommend** one option to the business, justifying why that *one single option* is far more beneficial to the business than any other option.

Each question requires more from learners in terms of their depth of knowledge. Also each question requires a more developed and detailed response than the one previous, so that learners have to gradually demonstrate higher-order thinking skills. The theory is that knowledge acquisition takes place gradually and in a step-by-step process. I have alluded to this earlier on, by referring to it as incremental. This notion was developed by educational psychologist Dr. Benjamin Bloom (1956), who advocated that simpler concepts had to be mastered before those that were more complex and challenging. Known as **Bloom's taxonomy**, six levels of thinking skills are divided into two categories which are lower-order and higher-order thinking skills.

Lower-order thinking skills	Higher-order thinking skills
Applying: Use previously learnt information within a given situation.	**Analysing:** Comparing two or more pieces of information and drawing a conclusion.
Understanding: Demonstrate understanding through **explaining** a theory or concept.	**Creating:** Showing creativity through presenting information in a different way, or inventing a new design, etc.
Remembering: Recall, state, suggest, define	**Evaluating:** Justifying a piece of advice based on critical examination of facts and theory.

The appropriate skills can be engaged by asking the correct type of questions.

Lower-order questioning	Higher-order questioning
What is ...?	What are the pros and cons of ...?
Can you define ...?	Can you suggest an alternative?
Can you explain ...?	Can you recommend and justify ...?
True or false?	What are the implications if ...?
Can you provide another example of ...?	What would happen if ...?
	What are the causes of ...?

Bloom's taxonomy has been widely adopted in education, not least by the exam boards. The importance of asking the right type of questions is not just so that learners can engage in the correct thinking skills, but so that they can familiarise themselves with the correct **command words** as adopted by the exam boards and reflecting the different levels of Bloom's taxonomy. By working with the appropriate command words on a regular basis, your learners will find that the words act as triggers for their memories and focus their minds towards providing a response of the correct level.

Some exam boards have a glossary of command words, explaining what level of response is expected per command word. This excellent resource is great for sharing with learners as it tells them exactly what the exam board is looking for in their response. Through this, learners can gauge how much time to spend on the question, the connectives to use, and the content to include, which will effectively allow them to meet the demands of the question.

The following is an extract from the Eduqas exam board This is extremely helpful to use as the basis of discussions and planning activities before learners actually attempt a question:

"If you are asked to **suggest** something then you should **put forward a possible idea, reason or course of action.** There is no requirement to expand on the suggestion(s) you have made, unless you are asked to do so. An example of the type of question that you might come across include:

Suggest three ways that a business could increase productivity of its staff."

On evaluation

"......... **make a judgement based on weighing up points for and against** that which you are asked to evaluate. In your response, you should **provide a verdict as to what extent you agree with a statement**, on the basis of presenting evidence and examples taken **from a wide range of sources** that both agree with and contradict the statement......."

"**Evaluate** the impact of Economic and Social factors on a business."
(www.eduqas/assessment_objectives.com)

Links can be made between the assessment objectives, the lower-order and higher-order thinking skills, and the command words. All three have to be aligned with each other for rigorous assessment that is consistent with the exam board criteria. Assessment Objectives 1 and 2 would come under the lower-order thinking skills. Assessment Objectives 3 and 4 would come under the higher-order thinking skills. Through lower-order skills, learners can ground their knowledge and apply it to a given situation. Higher-order thinking skills allow learners to fully investigate the scenario, and demonstrate their reasoning, justification, and evaluative skills. For this to be successful, learners need to be provided with a variety of levels of learning throughout the duration of the lesson through which they are sufficiently challenged.

Adopting this approach further ensures that learners are provided with opportunities to progress within a lesson. Moreover, at various points within the lesson, as well as at the end of the lesson, learners are able to demonstrate the level of progress that they have made from when they first arrived. For this to occur, consistently using command words, as used by the exam board, allows learners to become familiar with the language and expectations of what the question or scenario demands. To support learners in being able to achieve this, the objective of the lesson could simply be to "explain and analyse," whereas for other lessons it could be to "analyse and evaluate." This will be dependent upon learner needs as well as the length of time that is available in the classroom/on the course. With awareness of your learners and their learning needs, you will be able to devise appropriate activities that allow them to become familiar with the assessment criteria, and, as learners become familiar with these concepts and they progress on the course, there is no need to teach these concepts independently of any real learning.

Assessment, in line with assessment criteria, becomes as important and complex as the acquisition of new knowledge and information by learners, which needs to be checked through the responses that they provide to the activities and questions that you have set. To ensure rigour of assessment, questions posed to learners can be actual exam questions from past papers, or in the style of exam questions for which you have produced a mark scheme that is similar to that provided by the exam board, illustrating the criteria they need to meet to achieve the allocated marks. Asking learners to provide responses that meet criteria for Assessment Objectives 2, 3, and 4 when they have just been introduced to new content can be challenging. However, optimum learning experiences are those that allow learners to feel challenged and just out of their comfort zone. At this level, learners are more likely to engage with the learning material, and

so it is better to have higher expectations of learners a
accepting their complacency and allowing them to coas

Therefore, although you may devise an activity or se
order of the assessment objectives, some learners may feel
and activities that assess lower-level skills and knowled;
differentiation (see Chapter 6 "Learning and Teaching
that learners have the option to select the activity that th
This empowerment is more likely to motivate learners
working harder to meet the demands of the assessment
criteria. With this in mind, learners may not necessaril
that demand responses reflective of their target grade as learner ability ...
with new material will dictate which activity they strive to complete.

For example, low-ability learners and those who are not confident with the new
learning material may want to complete the questions that require them to meet the
skills and knowledge required at Assessment Objectives 1 and 2, so that their learning
and confidence with the new content is incremental, and more suited to their learning
needs and preferences. Activities that require learners to work with their peers, or are
scaffolded to allow learners to achieve the assessment criteria boundary consistent with
their target grades is a good strategy to use to motivate learners so that they strive a little
harder to work at the level that is consistent with their ability.

In a similar vein, verbal activities that allow learners to express their learning while
presenting their ideas to the rest of the group can be quite effective too, especially
if there is a requirement for peers to make positive suggestions of where learners are
doing well and where improvements can be made, and how they would improve
learner responses. This will require some preparation as you will have to set the criteria for the level of learning, as well as grade boundaries. These will enable learners
to take on the role of both the learner and the assessor, and in doing this, learners will
have to use the language in the criteria and grade boundaries to justify their responses.
Not only does this allow learners to illustrate their ability to be able to demonstrate
their understanding of the assessment criteria, but it allows you to assess the level
of their own understanding. The significance of this is that it can catapult their skill
level through which they are able to provide better responses to exam-style questions.

Explain what e-commerce is, give examples of some businesses that you know that use e-commerce. (2) **AO1, AO2** Explain your understanding of the business and its products so far. (2) **AO1** Using examples, analyse in detail the benefits and drawbacks to the business of using e-commerce to promote its products. (6) **AO3** Should this business seek to achieve growth through e-commerce activities? With detailed explanation, say whether or not you agree with this idea. (6) **AO4**	A local home-grown business manufacturing 100% recyclable disposable dishes has experienced exponential growth. They are now looking to take this growth worldwide. They feel that, with the world focused on ditching the use of non-recyclable plastic, they need to sell their products globally through their very own dedicated website. Evaluate the consequences to this business achieving growth through e-commerce. **(16) (AO1, AO2, AO3, AO4)**

From the above example, it can be seen that learners who need a more incremental approach can engage in the same level of assessment as those who have the ability

...ectively to an essay-style question, avoiding boredom and disengagement. ...support learners, they can discuss their responses in pairs, and then write the ...down. For maximum impact, once learners have discussed their responses with ...peers, they could provide written responses independently under timed conditions. ...is not only tests their skills and knowledge but allows them to build on their timing too.

The plenary provides the final opportunity to engage with the assessment criteria. *Do not underestimate the power of the plenary.* This is your final assessment point! The purpose of the plenary is to measure the level of learning that has taken place for the duration of the lesson. The criteria that you would apply at this stage is whether or not learners have accessed the learning, and to what extent. For this to be effective, due consideration must be given to the plenary in your planning. Even though it is the final activity of the lesson, it must be rigorous. The reason for this is that it enables you to clearly identify whether or not the correct level of learning has taken place and it allows you to plan effectively for the next lesson. Aim high and ask questions that will engage higher-order thinking skills. To make sure the correct questions are asked, questions may need to be pre-planned so that they are asked in the correct order, to the correct learners, and that learners are provided with the best possible opportunity to demonstrate their knowledge acquisition.

Another possibility is to plan individual activities such as:

> Your friend has missed the lesson and sent you a "Snapchat" asking about what you did. Send him/her a quick reply *evaluating how pricing decisions will affect a business and its stakeholders.*
> *(Learners need to discuss: revenue, turnover, profit, competitors, industry average, etc. Ask them to group stakeholders instead of talking about them individually.)*
> Here, learners can provide short and snappy responses that succinctly demonstrate their understanding of the topic.

So, the way in which assessment criteria is used varies according to the level and type of learning you are assessing. It is not a singular thing that is approached at the end of the course, which would be an extreme form of summative assessment. Neither is it of just one type or another. Nor is it applied at just one point in the lesson or at strategic points throughout the duration of the course as a method of formal, or summative, assessment. Rather it needs to be a genuine assessment for learning, varying all the while to meet the assessment requirements of the topic and the needs of the learners. It is a fluid and continuing element of the teaching and learning cycle, which is consistently implemented. Small steps are taken every lesson to allow learners to sufficiently meet the assessment criteria at a level that effectively reflects learners' capabilities.

Reflection point: Consider a class that you have observed or have taught:

1　How did the lesson end?
2　What did you know about what the learners had learnt at the end of the lesson? How do you know?
3　What did the learners believe that they had learnt? How do you know?

Resources

There are many resources that you can use to pitch your lesson at the right level. They come in many formats - from textbooks (electronic and hard copy) and activity sheets to workbooks - that learners can work through on individual topics. Many schools and colleges prefer to use exam board–endorsed textbooks. This is because the information and activities they contain are usually tailored to the requirements of the specification. The style of questioning and marks awarded per question tend to reflect the style and type that could be found in the exam. Another feature of these resources could be that they have end-of-unit assessments, sometimes with suggested answers that you could use with your learners. This not only relieves you of having to think of a scenario that learners can apply their knowledge to and find the answer to, but also provides you with a suggested response that you can share with your learners. Furthermore, it allows you the flexibility through which you can break up the activity and only use part of the activity as a formal assessment to suit the time you have available per lesson. You could choose to link some of the questions to the learning objectives of the lesson and use them as classwork or reinforce learning and use them as homework, which you can check skill and knowledge. This may only leave a couple of questions that meet the needs and the purpose of the assessment as assessment questions. This is fine as it is the most efficient use of the assessment activity and the time that you have - both in terms of lesson time and marking time, should you wish to mark the assessments yourself.

However you wish to use the assessments, as answers are provided, you can familiarise yourself with the assessment criteria beforehand in order to support a more fluid structure to the lesson. Further, you can tailor revision sessions and provide guidance to your learners of what the expectations of them are in terms of the responses that they provide as part of this assessment. Once the assessment is complete, the guide could be used to allow learners to peer mark each other's work. The benefits of this is that learners can gain experience of trying to match each other's work with the criteria, and in attempting to do so learners can see where their strengths are and where errors were made. Seeing how omitting key words can make a big difference to the final mark and can enable them to become more proficient in working towards meeting the requirements of the assessment criteria.

To assess the level of progress, and indeed, if progress is being made at all, questioning is used throughout and/or at strategic points of the lesson to allow learners to provide evidence of their learning. This assessment benefits both teachers and learners. For teachers, they can assess whether knowledge acquisition is sufficient to meet the requirements of the specification and the skill level is sufficient to respond appropriately to the assessment criteria. As learners are placed under the spotlight, language that is consistent with the assessment criteria is best to use. Once you have gained this insight into learners' knowledge, you can prepare to assess them again in a different format.

If learners can evidence their knowledge at the correct level, which is in line with their target grades, then they can begin to feel confident that they are making sufficient progress at the correct level. This can be a motivating factor for them and can instill confidence in them that they *do* have the skill and ability to be able to succeed in the exam. Therefore, all the learning is worthwhile. This confirmation can further assist learners in becoming more motivated and taking ownership of their learning by consistently striving to achieve their goals and targets. Learners lean on this desire for success to consistently remind themselves of the assessment criteria through which they can illustrate their written skills and knowledge, self-assess, and peer assess. This is another way for them to practise their skills in meeting the needs of the assessment criteria. To some, this may seem rather monotonous, but as indicated earlier on, learning is a mixture of re-cap, acquiring new information, discussion, activities, assessment, and re-cap several times over again.

Knowledge acquisition, activities, starters, and plenaries are the aspects that allow creativity and variations in learning methods that will meet the learning needs and styles of learners. Scaffolds, or other support, by way of exemplars may need to be provided to those learners who need support in meeting the assessment criteria. You can use your creativity in this by providing differing support methods such as:

- Part Responses. To provide a response to a question that is started off by yourself/ peers and ask learners to complete.
- Word Banks. A list of words or phrases that are used to fill in gaps in a piece of text. This allows learners to quickly grasp the clear meaning of the word and the context it can be used in.
- Paired/Group Discussions. To plan responses prior to writing individually. This is usually for higher-mark questions, where learners are asked to provide responses that require evaluative/justification skills.
- Key Words. To provide clues of what key words/key terms to include in the response.
- Connectives. To provide a list of connectives that learners could use to enhance their responses.
- Estimation. To estimate how many lines the response should be. This indicator not only assists with the length of response, but it guides learners towards the length of time they should spend on other questions too.
- Exemplar Response. A response to a similar question is provided to learners that they can study for a limited time, prior to providing their own response.
- I Spy. Learners draft a plan of response individually, which is then edited and added to by another learner.
- Silent Planners. Learners work in pairs to write a response but without talking.
- Exam-style Questions. Learners write their own exam-style question and devise their own mark scheme. Then, they ask their peers to answer the question and assess it.

So, assessment does not have to be monotonous and tedious. It can have a creative element to it through which learners can gain the skills so that they can become better at meeting the assessment criteria. The more varied that this is, the greater the familiarity, and the better the acquisition of the material through which learners can provide a response.

Reflection point:

1　Are the assessment objectives ones that are transferable to "real life"?
2　Can you develop learner skills in working with the assessment objectives to have a greater relevance to the world beyond the classroom?

Regular assessment

One way of assessing if learners are making sufficient progress is through providing ample assessment opportunities. Instilling regular assessment in your lessons can be difficult, as the choice between progressing with new content and assessing depth of previously learned material can be a difficult task due to the limited time you have. Regular and continuous assessment is important in keeping learners reminded of the assessment criteria and the skills needed to demonstrate the learning that they have acquired. The more frequent the assessment, the more prepared learners can be for the final exam.

It is true to say though that if the assessment criteria is not met at the right standard, then it can be a waste of both the teachers' *and* learners' time, which is not only valuable but limited! Many schools have one formal assessment point every half term. There is a growing trend in making these cumulative assessments, which are a reflection of the exam. These include a variety of questions that test previously gained knowledge and knowledge that is learned more recently. This format of interleaving is crucial in ensuring that learners actively use previously learned material and engage with it frequently, so they don't learn a topic and "park it" in the back of their minds until a few weeks before the end of the course.

As all GCSE and A Level courses are now being assessed at the end of two years, learners need to be reminded of the topics that they have learned at the beginning, in the middle, as well towards the end of the course. Learners also need to be reminded of the variety of ways through which questioning will take place in the exam and can continue to build on the skill under timed and test conditions. Returning to previously learned topics allows learners to build the depth of knowledge they have, make links with other topics, apply their knowledge to differing situations, and begin to draw conclusions from it through which they can gain the confidence to respond to differing assessment methods, which can be at a variety of different levels. This skill is extremely important for A Level courses, as most specifications will have a synoptic question/synoptic paper. This means that all of the material within the specification will be tested within a single paper. Therefore, interleaving should be used to carry out regular assessments to ensure that all topics are assessed at all levels during the duration of the course.

Example of the format of an interleaving assessment

Assessment 1	Assessment 2	Assessment 3
Topic 1 – 50%	Topic 3 – 35%	Topic 5 – 25%
Topic 2 – 50%	Topic 4 – 35%	Topic 6 – 25%
AO's 1 & 2	AO's 1, 2, & 3	AO's 1, 2 & 3
	Topic 1 – 15%	Topic 3 – 15%
	Topic 2 – 15%	Topic 4 – 10%
	AO's 1, 2, 3 & 4	AO's 1, 2, 3 & 4
		Topic 1 – 15%
		Topic 2 – 10%
		AO's 1, 2, 3 & 4

Above is an example of the format of an interleaving assessment. Some would argue though that knowledge that is recently learned will be better answered, so less of that should be assessed than knowledge previously acquired. Whatever the method of interleaving you decide to adopt, the template above is a guide to direct you with that.

Keeping a record of what has been assessed and the resources that were used to carry out the assessment are a good way of ensuring that a variety of topics are assessed in a variety of different ways and that learners are continually assessed at the right level. Planning such assessments in advance can allow you to think about the method, the content, the duration, and the style of questions. Past paper questions are the ultimate resource for most of us. They are extremely beneficial in that not only are they devised by the exam board, but they should have a suggested response too. This is extremely useful to you as a trainee teacher who is trying to familiarise yourself with the complexities of assessment and the assessment criteria, but it is also useful for learners as they have the information in black and white of what the examiners are looking for.

Support is available online too from organisations such as www.tutor2u.net, who not only provide learning resources, but also provide activities and assessments with suggested answers. Their student-friendly resources are really useful, as they are engaging and challenging, and they can be used either as part of a formative and formal assessment, or as an informal but still formative classroom activity. They further use other social media apps to communicate updated material with teachers and learners, which makes them extremely accessible.

All of this preparation is to assist learners to gain confidence in demonstrating their skills and knowledge to the examiner. This is an extremely important process and must be taken seriously, as the only interaction that learners have with the people who will decide their fate is through providing written responses to a series of questions. The quality of responses will dictate the outcome of their qualification, which will stay with them for the rest of their lifes. Therefore, despite the argument that this could lead to boredom, low esteem, and de-motivation, it is absolutely crucial that learners practise the skill of meeting the assessment criteria to the best of their ability in order to be able to achieve the highest marks possible for the responses that they provide to the examiner. Just as sportspeople train to practise the skill for their sporting activities on a regular basis, so too must learners practise explaining, applying, and drawing conclusions from or evaluating their learning regularly. This learning must be assessed by both teachers and learners. Learners must know where they have made errors, and more importantly how they can improve so they avoid making the same mistakes over and again.

Conclusion

Assessment criteria is largely thought of as the tool through which learner progress is both measured and monitored. However, the far reaching impact of assessment criteria is much greater and valuable than this. It's role in the effective, purposeful and holistic delivery of the course should not be undermined. Consistently striving to meet the various levels of assessment criteria can allow you to plan and prepare purposeful lessons which are engaging and fully focused on learner progress and development. Sharing the skill and knowledge of how the demands of assessment criteria can be met and practicing it often so that learners become familiar with it making improvements as they go along, can also prove to be a motivating factor through which they are more engaged with the learning material and their overall achievement on the course.

Bibliography

AQA (on-line). Available from www.aqa.org.uk [Accessed 21 January 2019]

Eduqas (on-line). Available from www.eduqas.co.uk [Accessed 21 January 2019]

Further reading

Bloom, Benjamin and David R. Krathwohl (1956). *Taxonomy of Educational Objectives*. New York: Longmans, Green.

Black, Paul and Wiliam, Dylan. (1998). *Inside the Black Box: Raising Standards through Classroom Assessment*. London: NferNelson.

Kidd, Warren and Czerniawski, Gerry (2010). *Successful Teaching 14–19, Theory, Practice and Reflection*. London: Sage Publications.

Kolb, David A. (1984). *Experiential Learning Experience as a Source of Learning and Development*. Englewood Cliffs, NJ: Prentice Hall.

6

LEARNING AND TEACHING STRATEGIES

Differentiation

- An introduction to what differentiation is and why it is important
- Current priorities in education
- Understanding learning: understanding the adolescent
- Different approaches and practical examples

  - Whole-class differentiation

- Differentiation for learners with specific needs

  - Disadvantaged learners
  - Differentiating for learners with SEND
  - Gifted and able or high attainer learners
  - Twice-exceptional learners, i.e. gifted and with SEND
  - Learners with English as an Additional Language (EAL)
  - Literacy

- Differentiated learning objectives
- Differentiation within enterprise events
- Conclusion

An introduction to what differentiation is and why it is important

There is a story of a group of Māori (in New Zealand) having to cross a fast-flowing river. There was no bridge and if they crossed by themselves then there was a risk that some would be washed away. The method they developed to enable everyone to get across safely was to use a large log, which everyone held onto with the tallest and strongest at either end. That way, the entire group managed to cross the river.

If we applied the story of the group of Māori having to cross the river to education this might mean that all of our teaching would be undertaken in mixed-ability classes, with the more academically able learners having to take some responsibility to ensure that others in their mixed-ability class are able to achieve so that all attain to the same standard. However, much of education takes a different approach. We see that those who are particularly able in Maths or English are put into ability streams. Those who are good at Science are directed to Triple Science GCSEs. To study A levels, learners will be expected to have achieved a certain level of education - five GCSEs at Grades 1 to 4 (what were five GCSEs at Grades A to C). There is a good reason for this, which is that we want to see every learner achieve to their full potential. For the able, this may mean working and being challenged by those of similar ability. Those who were less able would obtain additional support.

While Business and Economics teachers will find that all of their classes are of mixed ability, there is still the expectation that all learners within the class are able to reach their potential academically and to go on to take their place within society, particularly from an economic point of view. To achieve this, every learner has to be taught in a way that will provide suitable stretch and challenge and/or support that matches their academic ability and overcomes barriers to learning, such as the learner for whom English is an Additional Language (EAL) or who has a Special Educational Need or Disability (SEND), or by taking due account of their starting point from the end of primary school. The technical phrase for this is **differentiation**.

Mixed-ability teaching does bring challenges, although the most significant is usually the implicit illusion that the following is true:

- Those who need support are less able.
- The more able will be held back by working with those who are less able or who have other barriers to learning.
- The less able learners will be unable to keep up with the more able learners.
- Learners are unable to change as they mature, as their circumstances change, and as their motivations develop.

As I visit schools and colleges, what I see is that those teachers who have consistently high expectations for *all* their learners and teachers who are prepared to lead them beyond the confines of the specifications, are also those who are most consistently successful in enabling ALL their learners to achieve highly as measured by their final grades.

Along with **Assessment for Learning**, the introduction of adapting our teaching to meet the needs of a variety of learners in our classes (differentiation) has marked a significant change in the way we view learners. In Business classes, this is particularly important as the option to stream the classes is not available, and our aim is to ensure that all are able to achieve their potential at that point in time.

Reflection point:

1   How do you feel about teaching mixed-ability classes?
2   Before we look at how to manage the learning in such classes, what do you expect of your learners?
3   Do you expect that they will all achieve the same grades?
4   Do you expect them all to have a sense of achievement at the end of the course?

Current priorities in education

As already indicated, there has been a significant change in the expectations for learners and, therefore, for those who teach them. Much of this reflects our national political and economic context, as well as developments in our understanding of learning. These developments are reflected in the recognition of national priorities to ensure that all learners are able to learn effectively. Consequently, both schools and individual teachers are expected to not only identify which learners may face barriers to their learning, but also how to adapt their teaching in order to address these challenges. At one time these priorities were identified as the disadvantaged (those pupils in receipt of the pupil premium), those with Special Educational Needs and Disabilities (SEND), English as an Additional Language (EAL), as well as literacy, numeracy, and behaviour. There was considerable work undertaken to develop individual strategies to address each of these, with many becoming identified as good teaching strategies for all learners. At the time of this writing, issues such as teacher workload, mental health, and particular SEND students with disabilities, such as autism and sensory deficiencies, are being highlighted as current priorities. Being aware of what the current priorities are as you are developing your teaching role will provide you with a basis from which to continue to develop your expertise in your career.

Understanding learning: understanding the adolescent

From the early-twentieth century, there has been an explosion in the interest in the way learning takes place. More recently there has been an increased expectation that how teachers teach is based upon research-evidenced practice. At this point, what is clear is that no single theory has all the answers, but rather that learning is a complex activity and understanding how we learn should have an impact on how we teach within the classroom. While there is a huge amount that we can learn from skillful practitioners, copying what they do is unlikely to enable a person to become equally skillful in a range of contexts. It is, therefore, important to be able to investigate different theories of learning and apply them critically in the situation you are teaching in. It is impossible to provide a broad and in-depth analysis of the range of theories that exist. The following can only whet your appetite to investigate further.

In the early part of the last century, **Lev Vygotsky** (1896–1934) recognised that learning is often a social exercise. Where those social interactions are managed well then learning can be constructed effectively. The theory was developed and became known as **social constructivism**. Two concepts underpin the theory; the **zone of proximal development (ZPD)** and the **more knowledgeable other (MKO)** (Pritchard, Alan and Woollard, John 2013). The ZPD is a way of describing that we learn best when what we are learning builds on what we already know. The closer the gap between the current and new knowledge then the easier it is to learn the new knowledge.

For example, at school we had to learn all the states and capitals of Australia. For many this was quite a task, as it was new knowledge and was not really connected to anything else in their memory. For me it was very easy. My mother is Australian and I already had an awareness of the different states and some of the capitals of those states. So, my ZPD was smaller than some of my friends and the gap between current and new knowledge was small. The wider application of this is in the development of **scaffolded learning**. For example, making links between lessons or having learning objectives that become increasingly difficult within a lesson can mean learners are able to achieve the most difficult learning objectives having gone through the stages identified in the earlier learning objectives.

The MKO is usually identified as the teacher in the classroom, i.e. the person who has more knowledge than those who are being taught and is able to skillfully scaffold that knowledge. However, in recent years there has been an increased awareness that the MKO may be another learner. So, the use of peer tutoring, small-group work, and jigsaw learning can aid the effectiveness of teaching, as well as reduce the burden for the teacher of being the centre of attention throughout the lesson.

While Vygotsky was developing his theory in Russia, **Jean Piaget** (1896–1980) was studying his own children and saw that they were able to learn in different ways according to their levels of maturity. His theory became known as the **Theory of Cognitive Development** or **cognitivism** (Schunk, D. H., 2012), and is reflected to some extent in the differing expectations of learners at the various Key Stages. The detail of his work is relatively limited in its application to the 14–19 age phase, as his work was with younger children. However, young people do mature over time and our expectations of how they engage with material will vary. For example, teaching Ethics to a year 10 group can be very different from teaching a year 13 group. Usually, a year 10 learner will still view the world in black-and-white terms. Dealing with questions that require a range of perspectives is difficult for this age group and discussion can be quite limited. However, by the end of year 13, learners should be able to provide a more nuanced discussion - not only identifying a range of factors to be taken into account, but also a variety of perspectives on those factors.

Many will have heard of **Ivan Pavlov** (1849–1936) and his experiments with dogs. As the dogs made the connection between an external stimulus (a bell) and food they would salivate when the bell was rung. This was called **Classical conditioning**. **B. F. Skinner** (1904–1990) developed these ideas and applied them to people, developing his **Theory of Operant conditioning**, which in due course became part of the wider area of learning theory called **behaviourism**, where external stimuli will result in specific behaviour in people (Jarvis, P. et al 2003). Therefore, there is already an inbuilt expectation that certain behaviours are beneficial for learning and others interrupt learning. This has already been raised within Chapter 4, "Learning and Teaching Strategies: Assessment for Learning," which introduced us to how this has been used within Assessment for Learning and explains the use of an objective-led curriculum. It has also been associated quite closely with the development and use of behaviour policies within schools, where both positive and negative reinforcement can be used to persuade learners to behave in ways that support their learning positively. This approach can be used in quite nuanced ways - learning how to promote behaviour in quite subtle ways, such as the use of praise or not rewarding poor behaviour so learners are able to develop behaviour patterns that lead to success. On the other hand, there are those who argue that this approach has quite a mechanistic view of people, i.e. we are like machines responding to specific stimuli.

Metacognition has gained attention in schools in recent years. John H. Flavell's (1979) **Theory of Metacognition** continued to be developed through the 1980s and can be summarised as having an awareness of our own thought processes. There are different aspects to this, such as our perception of our own abilities, or of the level of difficulty of a task, or the strategies we use to develop our knowledge and understanding. One development from this understanding of how we learn has been that of **concept mapping**, where connections between topics can be explored visually. There are a number of different approaches, which go beyond the use of spider diagrams and can develop learners' skills in both literacy and the knowledge and understanding of topics. Often it is easier to identify the gaps in a learner's metacognitive ability rather than understanding the scaffolding needed to bridge the gaps.

One approach to developing that scaffold is the use of **interleaving**, which was described in Chapter 2, "Getting Started: Teaching Academic Subjects." As was clear within that chapter, interleaving is not just a case of a recapping at the start of a lesson;

it is enabling learners to engage with the same material in different ways and at different times. This approach allows for deep learning of the subject material, so that learners are not only able to recall the concepts, but they are also able to transfer that knowledge and understanding to different contexts. The skill of application – being able to apply theories of motivation, for example, to different business scenarios – along with skills of analysis and evaluation are intrinsic to the success of learners in the courses you will be teaching. Consequently, your own understanding and ability to apply this concept in different teaching contexts is key to your own success.

In 1988, **Carol S. Dweck** published her work where she identified characteristics in young children that would enable her to predict their ability to succeed in later life. What she had found was the ability to defer gratification in order to obtain a greater reward would predict that children would have the necessary resilience to keep addressing a task they found difficult in later life. More recently Dr. Dweck has been able to identify strategies that can be used to develop this attitude, which she named the **growth mindset**. In particular, developing an approach where hard work and persisting at a difficult problem is praised rather than just praising the final achievement will enable learners to achieve more in the long term. Where achievement is praised when learners have not worked for this, or if learners feel that their hard work is not recognised then they will struggle to overcome difficulties. While this approach nominally has gained popularity, there are complaints that it is often poorly applied.

For a number of years, many schools latched onto the idea that we have a preferred way of learning, i.e. through images, by hearing, by reading, or kinaesthetically (movement), or perhaps using another sense often referred to as **VARK Modalities**. (VARK stands for Visual, Aural, Reading, Kinaesthetic.) The original ideas, which come from **Neil D. Fleming and Colleen Mills** (1992), resulted in the development of commercial enterprises to train schools in the diagnosis of learners and mechanisms to enable learners to use their modality effectively. There have been many subsequent studies that undermine the view that we have a specific learning preference. However, it has also led to an increase in creativity in the classroom which has enabled learners to engage more fully in their learning.

More recent developments in the area of **cognitive neuroscience** have extended our understanding of how the adolescent brain develops and how this development impacts on how young people learn. The earlier work undertaken by Jean Piaget had been during a time when young people joined the adult world of work at a young age and it was assumed their brains had stopped developing. While teachers recognised that their learners changed significantly during their adolescent years, there had been no studies of how the brain changed during that time.

The work by **Sarah-Jane Blakemore** in 2005, using functional magnetic resonance imaging (fMRI) over a number of years, has provided deep insight into the brain's development and the impact on learners' ability to engage with their learning and the increasing complexity of what they study as they get older. In particular, significant changes regarding the prefrontal cortex (which governs the executive function of the brain, i.e. decision making), the amygdala (which governs emotions), and the nucleus accumbens (which governs behaviour related to seeking rewards) are identified. Often this is connected to learners' emotional development and their own management of behaviour. However, it also links to how teenagers learn as they are able to manage information more effectively and identify multiple perspectives. This research has provided scientific evidence that the differences between boys and girls in the classroom reflects what is happening inside their brains. It is not just a case of social conditioning or hormonal changes; girls' brain development is about 2 years ahead of boys.

There are many other learning theories that play into our understanding of our learners, such as **Howard Gardner's Theory of Multiple Intelligences** (1993). As stated at the start of this section, the aim is not to provide you with details about all Learning Theory. The aim is to whet your appetite to learn more, and to learn with a critical eye. You should not accept at face value what you are being told; you should review the theory in light of your own experience in the classroom.

Reflection point:

Consider what you were like when you were 12, 16, 18, and 21:

1   What did you like to do?
2   What was your attitude to study?
3   How did you relate to adults?
4   What changed during that time?
5   What is your approach now to something that you find difficult?
6   Can you think of someone who was at school with you but who failed to achieve?
7   How do the theories provide an explanation of your own experiences?
8   How do the theories help you as you consider the students in your classes?

Different approaches and practical examples

As we come to the part of the chapter that looks at strategies, the most important thing to know is that the better you know your class as a whole and your learners as individuals, then the better you will be able to teach them. As Business and Economics groups are not streamed, all of our lessons are mixed-ability and there is a need to ensure that our differentiation is both effective and efficient, i.e. effective so all our learners can reach their potential; efficient so they are not unnecessarily time-consuming to prepare and still have impact. The following approaches have been chosen to address these issues.

Whole-class differentiation

We are going to begin with those strategies that can be applied on a regular basis to the whole class and to a consistent standard. The one that is probably most underestimated for its impact is **differentiation by organisation**, i.e. how the class is organised both in terms of the setting out of tables, material on the walls, and where you seat the learners in your classroom. For example, it is known that those learners who are easily distracted, for whatever reason, will work best if they are facing the teacher, i.e. they are sat in rows or, if older, in a horseshoe shape. Going beyond this, the way in which learners are organised around the room will make a difference to their learning.

An early question to consider is how you are going to seat learners according to their academic ability. Are you going to have them "streamed" within your classroom so learners who have been identified as high attainers sit together or do you take an approach where you sit learners in mixed-ability groups? There are arguments for both approaches. Where you have learners streamed classwork can be set specific to the level of ability. Those learners who require additional support can be provided with this by the teacher, and those learners who are more able can be effectively stretched.

With a BTEC or vocational class this approach can be effective where learners can work on the same assignment tasks alongside each other and the teacher can provide appropriate levels of support (also known as **differentiation by task** and **differentiation by support**). However, in terms of efficiency this places a lot of demands upon the teacher to consistently develop separate materials that are appropriate to each group and to spread themselves between groups. Where this is not well managed it can lead to low expectations and a lack of challenge for learners. Moreover, it also fails to use a significant classroom resource, i.e. the learners themselves.

An alternative approach is to have mixed-ability groups. These allow learners to provide support to each other by sharing their understanding and skills. It has been argued that where learners are taught to provide appropriate mutual academic support then more able learners are able to develop a more profound understanding of their subject and less academically able learners are able to develop their knowledge and skills to a higher standard. The learning theory that is pertinent here is the more knowledgeable other (MKO) by Lev Vygotsky, which takes account of the significant role that a more knowledgeable person can have on someone else, i.e. to be able to extend his/her learning. It also keys into the adolescent brain, as during this time the importance of relationships with peers grows, which can mean that learners are more prepared to learn from peers than from adults. Just as is the case for having a class where learners are grouped according to ability, the key is managing the class so expectations are high for *all* learners. It is not automatic for mixed-ability groups to work effectively together so all learners achieve highly, but it is dependent upon training the group or groups to be effective.

Reflection point:

Consider one of your own classes and create learner profiles. Imagine this is a lesson on cash flow forecasting.

1 How would want to organise the physical space to maximise learners' learning?
2 How do you want to seat the learners? Who will you sit next to whom and why?
3 What resources might you want to develop?
4 What case studies/scenarios do you want to use that are appropriate to this class?

Another common approach is **differentiation by resource**. In this instance, it is not the development of a resource that will only be used within the single lesson, which is the normal approach to differentiation by resource. Rather this resource can be used regularly and without alteration, i.e. the development of *the learning mat*. This is a laminated handout with hints and tips to provide a scaffold of learning. For example, with a GCSE class you may want to produce some hints and tips that provide learners with ways to address 9 mark questions. Rather than generating different worksheets for every lesson for different learners, these laminated learning mats can be used every time you want your learners to develop an extended answer, even when not explicitly linked to exam technique. Not only would you develop different learning mats for different outcomes, e.g. extended answers, short answers, formulae for ratio analysis, etc., but you may want to have some learning mats with fewer hints and tips for those who are more able or as a way of reducing the scaffold as learners improve their skills. While this will engender some hard work in the short term, being able to use resources that can be used several times will ensure that you can spend time on other aspects of planning and delivery.

Other effective and efficient forms of differentiation are differentiation by support and differentiation by questioning. Both are very efficient, as once these skills have been learnt then the preparation time before the lesson becomes negligible. However, it is important to acknowledge that they are skills and have to be developed by considering them carefully. As differentiation is about supporting learners to be able to achieve highly by themselves, then the support given, and the type of questioning has to be such that both student knowledge and skills is scaffolded – not merely provided by the teacher.

Differentiation by support is when individuals or small groups of learners are provided with specific support from the teacher, or teaching assistant where available. The aim is to use tactical questioning to guide learners to a point where they can provide the right answer in an appropriate format. Sometimes this will be by providing additional guidance on where to find information, or the provision of a writing scaffold, or just by checking they understand what is being required of them.

This concept of differentiation by support is closely linked to differentiation by questioning. **Differentiation by questioning** begins with deciding which questions to aim at different learners. The simpler questions will be directed to those who have been identified as weaker with a concept. Often this is determined through the use of target grades identified by the school. However, as Business and Economics work with a wide range of topics, requiring different skills, it may be that an individual may be strong in one topic and weak in another. Using Assessment for Learning strategies will allow you to identify who is comfortable and who is struggling with this topic.

The simpler question may be to ask for a definition or an example of a key concept, e.g. What is one of the 4 Ps of marketing? (Price, Product, Place, and Promotion) By being able to answer this simple question, confidence with the subject is being built. Having ascertained the answer to this question, then a more difficult question can be asked, either of this individual or of someone with a higher target grade, e.g. What are different versions of this P?

So if the first answer was **Price**, the following question to another, more able student can be:

- *What are the different ways that pricing is used in marketing?* followed by…
- *What examples can be provided of when "skimming" has been used as a marketing strategy?* leading to…
- *What were the advantages of using this strategy?* And then…
- *What were the disadvantages?* And delving more deeply…
- *What about the ethics of this strategy?*
- *Was XX right to use this strategy? Why…?*

By using such a strategy, the class as a whole is developing the answer using each other's skills and abilities (social constructivism). Learners are being guided through different levels of thinking (Bloom's taxonomy). It builds skills, which are not only necessary for succeeding well according to exam criteria, but also addresses issues of morality, structured speaking, which develops oral communication, and can form a basis of written work (metacognition). Learners who are more able in this subject area are modelling good practice to other learners, who are then learning from their peers.

Having looked at a number of strategies that allow for effective and efficient differentiation, using research that informs those strategies turns our thoughts to strategies that address individual national priorities. This begins with pupil premium as the highest on the government agenda at this point in time.

Differentiation for learners with specific needs

There are a wide range of specific needs that learners may bring with them to their learning. It is always important to remember that the need should not define the person and the condition should not be used as a proxy for the name of the student. This may seem obvious, but it is surprisingly common.

Disadvantaged learners

Due to the continuing and growing gap between disadvantaged and advantaged children, in terms of achievement at school and opportunities following school, there has been a significant amount of work done to develop strategies and encourage schools to prioritise their work with this group of learners. This has included the publication of good practice case studies in *Special Educational Needs and Disability* (Ofsted, 2010), other reports, and even awards for those schools that achieve in this area.

The most significant work has been undertaken by The Sutton Trust and the Education Endowment Foundation and resulted in the *Teaching and Learning Toolkit* (EEF), which can be found here: https://educationendowmentfoundation.org.uk/ resources/teaching-learning-toolkit

The toolkit provides a list of more than 35 strategies – together with the measureable impact of each and their relative cost – and how much research evidence is linked to support these findings. The two strategies that have been identified as having the most impact for disadvantaged learners are feedback and the use of metacognition and self-regulation (sometimes called "learning to learn").

Feedback is a key concept within Assessment for Learning and is discussed more fully within Chapter 4 "Learning and Teaching Strategies: Assessment for Learning." In brief, it is feedback that is individualised for each learner and the work that each learner has completed. Feedback should provide clear support and direction against success criteria that the learner is then able to respond to. Schools have developed a variety of approaches to support this, such as the use of peer tutors and particular methods to show that learners are responding to the feedback provided. With these approaches, care has to be taken to ensure the marking load remains manageable and that learners are not overwhelmed by the feedback they are expected to engage with.

Metacognition uses approaches that allow learners to develop strategies that improve their memory of key concepts, make links between those concepts, and critique concepts in order to access higher-order thinking skills. As indicated earlier, examples include the use of learning maps and concept mapping. Both approaches require regular practice by learners and go beyond the use of spider diagrams, which have been prevalent in the classroom. In addition, the use of such strategies enables learners to engage in structured talk, whereby learners have to explain their reasoning to other students. This can be translated into written work and hence into improved exam results. This approach has also been shown to support other learners, such as those learners with speech and language needs. Interleaving is another way in which learners are enabled to engage with material in multiple ways in order to develop deep learning.

Differentiating for learners with SEND

Developing appropriate strategies for learners with Special Educational Needs and Disabilities (SEND) is now an accepted element of the role of the teacher. It is also underpinned by statutory requirements, such as the Special Educational Needs and Disability Act (SENDA) 2010, the Children and Families Act 2014, and equalities legislation including the Disability Discrimination Act 2005 as well as those defined by the Department for Education (DfE) Code of Practice.

SEND includes a wide range of learners. It is important to recognise that every learner identified with SEND is an individual and support mechanisms will need to be specific to that learner. The process will begin with assessing the learner's need and then developing approaches that are reviewed and evaluated on a regular basis to ensure that they are fit for purpose throughout the learner's education. Teaching staff will be required to work closely with the school SEND Coordinator (SENCo) and with a teaching assistant, when appropriate.

Where a learner has been identified as having particular needs - such as dyslexia, autism, attention-deficit/hyperactivity disorder (ADHD), or sensory impairment - approaches to teaching may need to be differentiated in a particular way for that individual. Dyslexia is usually identified in a learner as having difficulty with accessing the written word. Dyslexia can be seen when there is a significant contrast between a learner's good aural skills and the learner's written skills, which will be relatively worse. This may be because the writing shifts on the page as the learner tries to read it. Where this occurs some learners will benefit from the use of different coloured paper or use a different colour for the computer background. Pale blue is a commonly beneficial colour, whereas red print can be particularly difficult for a dyslexic to read.

Organisation can also be difficult for dyslexics, which will be seen in the way they process instructions or in how they set out their work, as well as having difficulties with spelling. Organisation of text can be made easier for such learners by the development of clearly structured handouts, with limited amount of text so words do not run into each other. In each of these examples, **differentiation by resource** is used, i.e. the resources are adapted in order to enable those learners to access the materials at their level.

As learners are different, how they present the characteristics of their learning needs will also be different. Therefore, how they will be supported is equally as varied. It is vitally important to discuss the support plan that has been developed with the SENCo and then experiment with the recommended approaches to identify which are the most effective. Alongside your own professional and critical evaluation of the approaches being used, discussing the approaches with learners themselves enables them to have a sense of empowerment over their own learning.

Gifted and able or high attainer learners

Working with those learners who have been identified as "gifted and able" learners or "high attainers" is an area many staff find challenging. It is worth noting that one element for such learners is the same as for all students, i.e. to encourage them to excellence and to refuse acceptance of less than this. A particular difficulty comes when teaching is "to the test" and there is little incentive for learners to do more than achieve the assessment objectives of the qualification requirements. To provide the context within which these learners can be challenged will mean they are expected to do *more* than the qualification requirements. This can be in relation to the tasks they are asked to complete, but also with the language they are expected to engage with and to use.

Developing tasks that go beyond the qualification requirements can be both stimulating and challenging for the new teacher – and can require a little imagination. I have seen recent Business graduates in their PGCE year incorporate degree level–style essays to be included within their planning of lessons and as a choice of homework for ALL their students. Where learners are studying for a BTEC Business qualification the tasks can be conflated to provide stretch and challenge, i.e. to both analyse and evaluate management styles or the roles of solicitors. Or it can be a case of providing a business simulation – perhaps by working with an employer. Developing a holistic approach to the delivery of the BTEC qualification often requires students to work with a higher level of challenge, as they have to synthesise information from different parts of the curriculum. Taking this approach may be beyond the opportunity available for a trainee or newly qualified teacher if a department is wedded to individual BTEC tasks, but it is hugely rewarding once you are in a position to develop this approach.

Use of language is about the spoken language teachers use and ensuring their vocabulary is not over-simplified, but a broad range of vocabulary is included. Learners love revealing their wordplay with their peers and it provides them with increased self-confidence. Language is also about the written materials learners engage with. A simple way of considering this would be to review the range of written materials that are used in lessons, e.g. the BBC website, *The Guardian, The Economist, Marketing Week,* as well as those case studies that are provided by the board or in textbooks.

Finally, it is always interesting to see the impact on the whole group of introducing strategies that have been developed for the "gifted and able" learners. Where you have a member of the staff who is prepared to challenge the stereotypes and resist the pressure of teaching to the test, the results can be impressive with not only the "gifted and able" learners attaining high results but other students achieving better than the target grades suggest. An example of this has been the use of the "silent debate" using an essay title as the starting point. Learners are paired up, with one member being tasked with arguing on behalf of the question and the other is required to argue against the question. The reason it is classed as *a silent debate* is because no words are allowed to be spoken. All arguments have to be written. Each member of the pair takes turns to write his/her argument; responding to the argument presented by his/

her peer and developing a new one. All learners engage with this with staff impressed at the quality of the end product and the passion with which some learners pursue their arguments.

Twice-exceptional learners, i.e. gifted and with SEND

Little material is available that specifically looks at strategies for teaching those who are both gifted/more able and also have Special Education Needs or Disability (SEND), and take into account the learners' perceptions. Where such research exists, there have been a number of interesting findings. One is the frustration they feel when their SEND acts as a mask of their giftedness and teachers do not plan effectively for their learning. Approaches that benefit such students include:

- Being given the choice in how to present their work.
- Having their work marked at a higher level.
- Working with experts.
- Having the opportunity to work at a different pace than their peers.

As for many learners, for these learners working in groups could be either a nightmare or an amazing learning experience, revealing that group work always needs to be carefully planned.

Learners with English as an Additional Language (EAL)

Increasing numbers of young people are arriving from Europe, Somalia, Iran, and Afghanistan, and most recently from Syria. While they are all identified as learners who do not speak English as their first language, it is also true that the reasons for their arrival has an impact on their integration into the classroom.

The young people may have come because their parents or carers are pursuing better employment opportunities and they may resent being brought here. They may be escaping from war and persecution and have significant emotional issues to overcome as well as adapting to a foreign culture with different educational expectations. They may have come to join a family or they may arrive in isolation. The most important aspect is that as the teacher you remember that they are young people who need to feel welcome in your class. You can show this by learning how to pronounce their name accurately, or by using a buddy system. Working closely with your SENCo the following are important questions that need to be addressed to begin to provide the support these young people need:

- How long have they been in this country?
- What is their first language?
- Have they been to school before?
- Can they write in their first language?
- Do they have any health or learning needs?

Support is available for the school from outside agencies who can provide an assessment of the child and provide additional input. However, the most effective method for English-language acquisition is by immersion, i.e. to be fully immersed within an English-speaking environment.

For those young people who speak very little English at the point of arrival it is not unusual for them to have a silent period of up to 6 months. Even though they are silent, they will still be learning, such as names, faces and places, basic communication skills, basic school vocabulary, the alphabet, and writing protocols. As they gain the confidence to speak in English they will still *think* in their mother tongue and, therefore, be constantly translating what they hear into their mother tongue and then having to translate their answer into English. Consequently, it is important to give thinking time as you wait for an answer to your question. By the end of 2 years, these learners will have basic academic language (during which time they are exempt from public exams). In 5 years, these learners should be competent in academic language and fluent in everyday English language.

To support language acquisition and assimilation into your classroom other practical strategies can be used. These include:

- Making available a dictionary in their mother tongue.
- Identifying key words in their mother tongue, which is written above the English word.
- Using pictures to support the text.
- Using matching activities so the words and phrases are already available.
- Asking simple questions.
- Using a simplified worksheet.

Further support for learning English as an Additional Language (EAL) is available through the National Association for Language Development in the Curriculum (NALDIC), which can be found here: https://naldic.org.uk/.

Literacy

While literacy is an aspect of learners' progress that many schools are addressing overtly with school-wide approaches, it is also the case that individual subjects will have issues that are specific for their area. The nature of our subject lends itself to providing a range of opportunities to develop both verbal and written literacy skills. However, the following have been identified as issues:

- Quality of language
- Spelling
- Learners writing as a consumer rather than as an employee.
- Applying understanding of new concepts is difficult.
- Learners showing limited use of business terms apart from when they are directly implied by the question.
- Limited ability to synthesise material across the subject.

The starting point for literacy within a subject is the teacher. It is the teacher's responsibility to model how to speak about the subject and how to write in ways appropriate to the context. The use of structured talk, writing frames, peer and self-assessment, and specific teaching regarding command words all provide strategies to address a number of the issues identified.

Differentiated learning objectives

A significant change in recent years has been the way in which differentiation is understood and implemented. It used to be the case that differentiation was so linked to expected achievement it was assumed that lessons would include learning outcomes that not all learners would achieve. This would be seen in Learning Outcomes that were set out as:

- **LO1.** All learners will be able to achieve this
- **LO2.** Most learners would achieve this
- **LO3.** Some learners would achieve this (i.e. only the most able)

This approach has had an impact on motivation of both the most able and those who were identified as not being able to achieve the final learning outcome. Recently the emphasis has moved in identifying strategies that enable *all* learners achieve *all* the learning objectives. It may be that not all of the learners will achieve each of the learning outcomes to the same level, but the role of the teacher is to devise strategies to support those who may struggle to achieve the final outcome as well as ensure that the brightest are stretched even with the learning outcome that looks easy to achieve. For example, using a selection of learning outcomes (LO) from a break–even lesson we may have:

LO 1: To be able to define break–even

This assessment activity will help me to identify those who may find this topic easier than others and is described as *differentiation by outcome*. As the first LO, all learners may be expected to achieve this to the same level.

LO 2: To construct a break–even table to identify the break–even point

Differentiation by organisation (seating plan). Using learner data on which Maths set they are in, I will have mixed "ability" grouping. Where the buddy system is working well, stretch and challenge comes from the manner of support the more able learners are providing to those who are finding later aspects of the task a challenge. This means everyone is able to achieve this LO, with the benefit for the more able learners that their literacy skills are developed and their understanding is deepened because they have to explain this to their peers.

Differentiation by outcome: Initial questions will have used simple questions, with whole numbers as answers and all learners will be expected to complete these. Further stretch and challenge will exist with additional questions contained on the worksheet where the answer is not a whole answer. Learners will have to decide what is the right answer and explain why.

LO3: To be able to identify and discuss changes in costs and/or sales revenue in the context of a case study.

Differentiation by organisation will continue to be used so that all learners are able to achieve this to some level. *Differentiation by differentiated questioning* can also be used, with more able learners expected to provide not only more detailed answers but to be able to justify their reasoning.

In Chapter 2 "Getting Started: Teaching Academic Subjects," using a single overarching objective was recommended as a way of ensuring that there are high expectations for *all* learners. Again, the support and/or challenge for individual learners would be differentiated so that all would be able to reach their potential, but all learners would be expected to achieve the objective.

Differentiation within enterprise events

Schools often have days when they collapse the timetable to provide their learners with different experiences that enhance their overall education. Business teachers are often asked to arrange enterprise events, in order to develop employability skills of their learners, such as team working, financial capability, creativity, and using initiative. Because this may be for a whole-year group during a single day or half day, the approaches used for normal classroom teaching may not apply. Although individual needs will still need to be taken into account, such as providing appropriately coloured paper for a dyslexic learner.

For such events, the dominant strategy will need to be *differentiation by organisation*. This cannot just be a case of creating mixed groups and hoping that everyone will get along and make a contribution. The groups and their activities will need to be planned and managed carefully to ensure that everyone will have a specific role to fulfill and it will tap into different skills that are expected to exist within the group. These may be along the lines of someone acting as a "resource investigator," i.e. someone who will be responsible for managing the resources. Another may be a timekeeper, i.e. the person who will take on the role of ensuring tasks are completed on time and encourage the team to work faster if need be. Moreover, the use of structured talk will also help learners to develop those wider communication skills that also will allow them to access higher levels of cognition.

Reflection point:

Consider the following brief for an Enterprise Day at a school.

"Design a trading day for Year 9 students, where learners work in small groups to produce a product that they then have to sell to the rest of the school."

Design an activity that could be used during the day and identify how to manage the groups so that every member of the group has a contribution to make.

Conclusion

Approaches to differentiation change over time as our understanding of how young people develop as well as external factors, particularly, how a school's performance is measured. Differentiation can, therefore, be as much an ethical question as a pragmatic one. Is it a case of ensuring that your class results suit the dominant school narrative, or is your approach more student-centred and governed by your own personal sense of professionalism? This may be influenced by your understanding of your role in the classroom - "sage on the stage or guide on the side." One approach will lead to seeing the class as a unit or a team, where the intention is for all to achieve excellence. The other is to see the class made up of individuals all requiring bespoke strategies to enable them to achieve their targets. Both are utopian and this chapter has sought to highlight not only some significant areas of focus but also the complexity of the role. Something that will support teachers as they seek to become better at their teaching of the subject is *assessment for learning,* which responds to the integrated nature of teaching. If the assessment strategies are good, then you, as the teacher, will understand the learning of your learners and you will be able to adapt your practices appropriately.

References

Blakemore, Sarah-Jayne (2005). *The Learning Brain: Lessons for Education.* Oxford: Blackwell Publishing.

Dweck, Carol S. (2006). *Mindset: The New Psychology of Success.* New York: Random House.

Department for Education (2015). Special Educational Needs and Disability Code of Practice: 0–25 years. Crown copyright DFE-00205-2013 (online). Available from: https://www.gov.uk/government/publications/send-code-of-practice-0-to-25 [Accessed 23 January 2019]

Education Endowment Foundation (2019). *The Teaching and Learning Toolkit* (online) Available from: https://educationendowmentfoundation.org.uk/resources/teaching-learning-toolkit [Accessed 23 January 2019]

Flavell, J. H. (1979). "Metacognition and Cognitive Monitoring: A New Area of Cognitive–Developmental Inquiry." *American Psychologist,* 34(10): 906–911.

Fleming, Neil D. and Mills, Colleen (1992). *Not Another Inventory, Rather a Catalyst for Reflection from To Improve the Academy,* Vol. 11, 1992, p. 137 (online). Available from: http://www.vark-learn.com/wp-content/uploads/2014/08/not_another_inventory.pdf [Accessed 23 January 2019]

Great Britain. Parliament (2014). *Children and Families Act.* London: Her Majesty's Stationery Office (HMSO).

Great Britain. Parliament (2010). *Equalities Act.* London: Her Majesty's Stationery Office (HMSO).

Jarvis, Peter, Holford, John, and Griffin, Colin (2003). *The Theory and Practice of Learning,* Second Edition. London: Kogan Page Ltd.

NALDIC The National Association for EAL (online). Available from: https://naldic.org.uk/ [Accessed 23 January 2019]

Ofsted (2010). Special Educational Needs and Disability Review. Manchester: Crown. Copyright (online). Available from: https://www.gov.uk/government/publications/special-educational-needs-and-disability-review [Accessed 23 January 2019]

Pritchard, Alan and Woollard, John (2013). *Psychology for the Classroom: Constructivism and Social Learning.* Oxon: Routledge.

Schunk, Dale H. (2020) *Learning Theories: An Educational Perspective,* 8th ed., London: Pearson.

Further reading

Flavell, John H. (1999). *Cognitive Development: Children's Knowledge about the Mind.* Annual Review of Psychology Palo Alto, (50): 21–45.

Gardner, Howard. (2006). *Multiple Intelligences: New Horizons in Theory and Practice.* New York: Basic Books.

Hendrick, Carl and MacPherson, Robin (2017). *What Does This Look Like in the Classroom? Bridging the Gap between Research and Practice.* Woodbridge: John Catt Educational Ltd.

Pritchard, Alan (2018). *Ways of Learning: Learning Theories for the Classroom,* 4th ed., Oxon: Routledge.

7

DEVELOPING WIDER SKILLS

Seeing beyond the specification

- Introduction – the place of skills development within the modern curriculum
- Business links – how to develop high impact low cost approaches
  - Learner links
  - Your links
  - Other businesses
  - Competitions
  - Capacity building
- Enterprise Education and enterprise events
  - A short history of Enterprise Education
  - Enterprise skills
  - Assessing enterprise
  - For the enterprise coordinator: what makes for successful Enterprise Education?
- Financial literacy
  - Curriculum requirements
  - Supporting materials
- Embedding higher-order skills development within the "ordinary" Business or Economics lesson
  - Using student knowledge – not your own
  - Starting with the case study – not the (exam) questions
  - Teaching without learning objectives
- Learner well-being
- Conclusion

Introduction – the place of skills development within the modern curriculum

A very capable learner was applying to Universities. One University asked her to submit a further personal statement where she was asked to explain a problem she had to overcome and how she had done this and linked to her A level studies. Despite studying three academic A levels at a high-performing sixth form college, it became apparent that she felt she was following directions rather than solving problems in each of her A level courses. In the end, the problem she addressed was how to write the personal statement within an academic context that relied on "spoon feeding" rather than academic challenge (with support). She wasn't offered a place.

The justification many subject teachers provide for their teaching to be dominated by "teaching to the test" is that it provides the gateway to further study or employment. To an extent this is true in that learners will achieve the entry criteria in terms of examination grades. However, what it doesn't do is to prepare them for the demands of that next step. Many staff will recognise this as they work with first year Level 3 learners who have done well at Level 2, but then struggle with the increased demands at Level 3. In Higher Education (HE), transition from Level 3 to the first year of degree studies has become an area of research in its own right, as new learners struggle with the removal of support networks, tightly scaffolded lessons together with the introduction of independent research skills, along with specific referencing and literacy skills. Employers too indicate that learners – whether from HE, Further Education (FE), or school – lack a range of soft skills that they need to integrate quickly into the workplace and allow them to flourish.

The views of employers appear to be able to gain some traction with government, such as through the Lord Young (2014) *Enterprise for All: The Relevance of Enterprise in Education*, sponsored by the Pearson Trust, which was welcomed by elements of the Conservative government. This led to the reinstatement of Enterprise Education as part of the Ofsted inspection criteria for schools. Following this, a survey report, "Getting Ready for Work" by Ofsted (2016), investigating Enterprise Education and work-related learning in schools identified a patchy picture in terms of schools' commitment and ability to deliver opportunities for learners to develop enterprise and other transferable skills. Even where those opportunities did exist, there was little in the way of assessing learner progress either in terms of learners' enterprise skills or of the impact on wider learning. Ofsted currently requires post-16 education to support learners to develop employability skills. An outstanding provider will be able to evidence this with learners achieving additional relevant qualifications. While results and destination figures will still be the main evidence for the success of education, there is an awareness that wider skills development is important for learners.

As well as the need for learners to develop skills for the "next step," whether that is for the next step of their academic development or for employment, the Department for Education (DfE) also expects education to support learners to prepare for their wider lives. For the Business and Economics specialist this is seen most clearly within the National Curriculum in learner development of financial capability as seen in both Citizenship programmes and in the new GCSE Mathematics courses. In this context, financial capability is firmly focused on personal finance, rather than business finance; although the Business/Economics teacher will still be expected to be the expert within this area.

The emphasis on personal finance and the exclusion of how business finance is managed appears to ignore the changing economic structure of the economy with an increasing proportion of those who are self-employed. About 14 percent of 18 to 30 year-olds are in the process of setting up their own businesses. Moreover, even within vocational programmes, the opportunities to acquire the skills of managing the finances of a business can be limited to coursework rather than to provide our learners with more tangible experiences that connect to real life. Ofsted (2016) itself indicates that education, in terms of schools and colleges, should be preparing learners to be employees. While we may not be able to change the curriculum of a school, we should recognise that as Business and Economics teachers we occupy a very privileged position in education in that we are able to build bridges between academic studies and the learners' wider lives. And rather than see this as a threat to learner achievement, the likelihood is that increasing learner engagement with the wider subject should lead to improved grades.

This chapter, therefore, seeks to identify specific initiatives and good practice in each of the following areas: business links, Enterprise Education, and financial capability. We will also be looking at how to develop some of those soft employability skills into the "ordinary" business lesson, and to make links between the academic skills of analysis and evaluation and the wider lives of learners.

Business links – how to develop high impact low cost approaches

Creating business links is great fun, engages learners, stimulates and enhances your own subject knowledge, has positive impact on results and later learner outcomes, and identifies the department as outstanding. Yet Ofsted identifies this as an area that is consistently underused. A significant reason for this is that teachers see the development of business links as time-consuming, both in terms of navigating school/college bureaucracy, as well as ensuring that the experience for learners will be good. Those departments that do work closely with businesses often do this as a result of qualification expectations, i.e. vocational qualifications. Working with a wide range of schools has allowed me to see many different approaches to developing business links. So what follows is a smorgasbord of ideas that have been used successfully, together with how departments have developed the capacity to do this.

Learner links

All learners have links to businesses. These are just some ideas to enable you to identify what those links are and how to enable learners to make links between course material and their own lives:

- Get learners to list five businesses they pass on the way home and identify the type of business that each business is, e.g. "One stop" owned by Tesco, is a public limited company (PLC); June the Florist is a sole trader; SPAR is a franchise. [This is particularly useful if you don't live in the area.]
- If learners in the class have part-time jobs, then discuss with them the terms of employment, rates of pay, contracts, etc. Discuss why these jobs are different. This discussion is great for the development of analysis and evaluation skills.
- Learners often have interests and hobbies that are businesses in their own right. e.g. the music industry. Learners could be tasked with identifying singers/bands in each category of the Boston Matrix and then justify their choices to the rest of the class.
- Get learners to interview someone they know who is an employee, a manager, or an owner of a business. Their results can either be written up or videoed on a phone to be uploaded to a shared area in school. Then discuss the results in class.
- Who are the entrepreneurs in the class/year/school? What do they do? Do they make a profit? If they are in your class, see if they will produce some accounts to share with the class.

- Who do learners follow on social media? Which businesses do learners buy from? Get them to follow business commentators of the main broadcasters, key businesses, and economic publishers.

Each of these not only fulfills specific specification/examination requirements, but each also provide you with market research on your own learners. You can then use the information to build your own case studies, or even get the more able learners to write the case studies for you. It is easy to set up, so it limits the impact on your own time.

Your links

As an individual you will have more business links than you probably realise - some of which are close at hand and easy to benefit from. Moreover, those that are delivered in-house reduces the time constraints and bureaucracy, which hinders the development of business links and provides you with a greater degree of control over delivery. Those that are not in-house but are local will mean that the employer engagement can be limited to a timeframe of up to half a day, reducing the need for staff cover.

- **School and school staff.** It is not unusual for teachers to use the school as an example for different concepts, e.g. getting learners to write an organisation chart and identify where matrix structures exist. This can be developed to be even more engaging if you arrange interviews with key members of staff and their roles. For example, I observed a brilliant class "trip" to the canteen in the afternoon, where the canteen manager was interviewed around the theme of stock management and control. Heads of departments, bursars, etc., could all be usefully inveigled into participating in lessons to bring aspects of the curriculum alive.
- **Work with the Careers department.** Research shows that contact with employers through careers talks in Year 10 has a bigger impact than those delivered in Year 11. They will have a list of employers who are keen to go into schools and deliver talks about what they do.
- **Friends who are in business.** Experience has shown that asking a friend to do a talk is less effective than if you can identify a problem for the learners to address. Your friend can provide a short introduction to the business and set up the problem, and then learners work on this using their business knowledge. It means your learners have the opportunity to communicate on a professional basis within the school setting. For your friend, it may be that he/she gains an alternative viewpoint on the issue that he/she has set up, or confirmation that his/her own ideas are the right ones.
- **Governors of the school.** Usually within the governors' body will be members who are in business and are keen to support the school. Examples of working with governors include the delivery of Human Resources (HR) - mock interviews, talking about their role in the business (job description, person specification, organisation), assessing final project presentations.
- **Businesses you frequent and are local.** The likes of Asda (www.Asda.com) and Tesco (www.Tesco.com) will have community link co-ordinators who will be very supportive. If you frequent a branch of a national chain of restaurants, you may find that they will provide a free drink or food if you take learners on a visit to the local branch (and which will be part of their marketing budget). An

interesting twist on this was the delivery of a lesson on supply and demand of Costa Coffee whilst visiting a Costa Coffee shop. Economics and Business learners worked together in small groups to develop the contrasting and complementary understanding of supply and demand (linked to A level assessment objectives) and then presented their findings – while still in the Costa Coffee shop.

- **Working with your Professional Association, i.e. the Economics, Business and Enterprise Association (EBEA).** They arrange an annual conference at the Bank of England pitched at A level.

Other businesses

There are a number of different approaches that teachers use to develop links with other businesses. In the first instance are the traditional trips that teachers often think of when the term business links is raised: visits to Alton Towers, Jaguar, Airports. Large businesses like these are used to having educational trips and will work with teachers to adapt to the requests of the school or department. The difficulty with these is that they are very popular and need to be planned early in the academic year, or maybe the previous academic year.

A number of teachers have developed effective links with their local **Chamber of Commerce** or the **Local Enterprise Partnerships**, where they exist. The most creative example I have come across is where the BTEC Level 3 Business was designed as a series of five projects. Each project was developed with a local employer from the local Chamber of Commerce and with the individual modules mapped across the projects. While a large amount of forward planning was required, the impact on the learners, the local community, and the reputation of the college was significant.

Other approaches to working with local employers include using them to support an Enterprise or employability event developed by the department. Occasionally, an employer will work with the department to develop a simulation of an actual challenge that the business had faced and students have to figure out how to address this issue. Where this happens, the common area of investigation is that of marketing, but human resources is another department worth considering.

The main business link development will be through the Head of Careers, particularly through **work experience placements**. Often documentation is produced by Careers for learners to record their experiences and for employers to make comments on the learners' experience. These can then be used by learners to inform their curriculum vitae (CV). By working with the Head of Careers to develop this documentation, connections can be made between the specifications and work experience.

With some qualifications, work experience is a requirement. In these instances, supplementary documentation for learners on these courses will be required. If formatting is consistent between the Careers documentation and the departmental documentation the result is perceived to be more professional, resulting in better engagement by both the employer and the learner.

Competitions

Competitions are a useful way of raising the profile of the department, as well as developing employability skills and increasing enthusiasm for the subject in the broadest sense. While they can be time-consuming, it could be argued that they are the most effective in terms of raising aspiration and enabling learners to develop transferable skills in a way that they are able to articulate in different contexts, such as on CVs or at interviews. The following are some examples of popular competitions, with weblinks included:

- "In school" competitions can be created to develop a range of transferable skills. An example of this was a competition for all Year 12 Business and Economics learners, BTEC, and A level. This ran over the last 3 weeks at the end of Year 12 and took place within scheduled lessons. Learners could work in groups of their own choosing and were all given the same brief. Each class undertook a peer review to identify the best team within that individual class. Each of the best teams from each group/qualification went on to compete against each other directly by presenting to a panel made up of a local employer and senior school staff.
- The Tenner Challenge. This is a free competition run by Young Enterprise and is for all learners aged 11–19. Each person registered is given a tenner from the Tenner Bank and has up to 4 weeks to use this to develop a business and run it. At the end of the 4 weeks, the learners keep their profits, but have to repay their original £10 plus £1 legacy donation. https://www.young-enterprise.org.uk/what-we-do/secondary-programmes/tenner/.
- BASE is the National Business and Accounting competition of the Institute of Chartered Accountants for England and Wales (ICAEW) for learners in school or college aged 16–19. Learners work on a specific business problem and are in competition with other schools, as well as teams within their school. It is designed to enhance employability skills, as well as encourage learners to think about a career in accounting. http://careers.icaew.com/campaigns/base-competition.
- The London Institute of Banking and Finance runs a Student Investor competition where learners work in small groups investing virtual money. There are significant prizes to be won by learners and the school. http://www.studentinvestor.org/
- My Kinda Future is an award-winning Social Enterprise that connects learners to employers who are looking for their next generation of talent. The company will arrange classes and "Insight trips," but they also work with businesses to set real-world challenges for learners to compete against each other with prizes, including work experience, guaranteed interviews, etc. https://www.mykindafuture.com/Educator
- The School Enterprise Challenge is an international competition where learners set up their own small business within school and is open to all ages. Set up by "Teach a Man to Fish," its aim is to encourage sustainability (so the business has to run for a period of time) and is owned by the school but run by the learners. The longer the business runs for and the more successful it is, the bigger the prizes become. http://www.schoolenterprisechallenge.org/about/about-us/.

Capacity building

Capacity is always an issue for teaching staff, as any initiative will take time to plan as well as to deliver. Different ways of addressing this have informed my choices above, e.g. using employers that you and your learners have easy access to either through locality or by personal engagement. This reduces the amount of time needed for planning.

Where learners are required to go offsite, then the time for this can be reduced to two hours or half a day by using local businesses, and the amount of cover required can be reduced. This may be further reduced if you are able to combine groups of learners, either across levels, such as GCSE and A level, or across qualifications, such as BTEC and A level Business or Business and Economics, or even across subjects, such as Business and Geography.

The amount of cover required can be managed by scheduling out of school visits at the end of the year, when Year 11 and Year 13 learners are on study leave or have left. Also Teaching Assistants can be used, if available.

If you are a school that is involved in the delivery of teacher training, then using the student teacher to take responsibility with the planning of employer engagement, under your oversight, is another way of developing capacity – as well as enhancing the student teacher's experience and modelling good practice.

Within the school, Careers Advisors will often have a remit to work with employers to enable learners to make informed decisions about their next steps, whether that is through the provision of work experience, or by inviting outside speakers. Working with Careers Advisors to find out which employers they are working with may expose areas of synergy, so working with a single employer can yield benefits for both the department and the school.

Reflection point:

Consider your teaching over the last term.

1　What was the most enjoyable aspect for the learners?
2　When were those points when your learners made connections between their own lives and what you wanted them to learn?
3　How can you improve the capacity for developing business links?
4　How can they be integrated into wider school planning?

This section has covered a lot of material, including both the traditional and the not so traditional understanding of business links. The intention is always to promote wider learning, to engage learners with the subject - and not just exam achievement - but still recognised as being dependent upon subject specialists to organise and deliver. The following section on Enterprise Education is an important part of the wider Business and Economics curriculum, yet common understanding of this is so vague that it is not unusual for school leaders to allow non-specialists to deliver this. As a consequence, Enterprise Education is not delivered either as effectively or successfully as it may be.

Enterprise Education and enterprise events

Enterprise Education should be an area whereby Business/Economics teachers are able to contribute to the wider ethos of the school using their subject specialist skills. Whilst many schools will not be very strategic in the way they approach Enterprise Education, they will still hold Enterprise days or events for their learners. For the Business/Economics teacher this should be your opportunity to shine.

For many teachers new to the profession becoming an enterprise coordinator can be their first step in developing their career beyond that of a subject teacher. This is because it gives them the opportunity to work across the school with different members of staff, as well as plan and deliver events that are not only enjoyable to learners, but if managed well can impact on wider skills development. This element of the chapter, therefore, seeks to provide an understanding of the background to Enterprise Education, and to give permission to you as the teacher to identify what skills your learners should develop, how to assess those skills and – if you get the opportunity – to develop excellent practice within the school.

A short history of Enterprise Education

As indicated within the introduction, Enterprise Education within schools has been inconsistently supported over the years. Under the Labour government, schools were funded to deliver Enterprise and Ofsted (2011) gave clear direction that it was intended to develop the employability skills of young people and improve their understanding of the economy, enterprise, finance, the structure of business organisations, and how they work. Ideally, Enterprise Education would involve whole-school provision to promote the economic and business understanding, enterprise and financial capability of all children and young people. In 2012, the Department for Education (DfE) decided to withdraw the statutory requirement to deliver work-related leaning at Key Stage 4, which included Enterprise Education. As a result, many schools withdrew their commitment to delivering this aspect of the curriculum. In 2014, Enterprise Education was reinstated as a (peripheral) element of an Ofsted inspection and led to the Ofsted (2016) report, "Getting Ready for Work," investigating Enterprise and work-related learning in schools, including work experience and employer engagement.

Enterprise skills

In the wide range of reports about Enterprise Education and organisations that deliver enterprise in schools there is no agreed definition of what Enterprise Education should include. The clearest guidance as to what should be provided in schools came from Ofsted (2011) and was described as **"the promotion of economics and business understanding and enterprise and financial capability."** Looking at the websites of two organisations that specialise in delivering Enterprise Education to schools, the only enterprise skills that they explicitly had in common were **communication** and **teamwork**. Two other skills they had in common in their individual lists were **resilience** and **problem solving,** although the terminology differed between the organisations. It can be argued that the inclusion of resilience both reflects and is a response to what appears in the national press around the theme of mental health of young people. It is an area that schools are trying to address. In contrast, problem solving is an attitude or skill that employers regularly identify within surveys as being a key employability skill. Within this, employers would include concepts such as using initiative, planning and organising, and analysing data. As can be seen, there is a contrast between what Ofsted would describe as Enterprise Education and the skills that are commonly delivered by organisations delivering enterprise and in response to school requests. It may be that this contrast reflects a lack of confidence in the subject matter and one which subject specialists should be in position to address.

This lack of an agreed definition of what Enterprise Education incorporates has meant that schools focus almost exclusively on the development of "soft skills" and "enjoyment" for their learners and a belief that anyone can deliver a good enterprise day or event. This provides an excellent opportunity for the Business/Economics department to be able to contribute to the development of an agreed definition of enterprise and what knowledge and skills learners are expected to develop, incorporating subject specialist expertise around those "hard" themes of financial capability, business and economics.

Assessing enterprise

Assessing enterprise and enterprise skills is addressed more fully within Chapter 4 "Learning and Teaching Strategies: Assessment for Learning," which identifies this element of the curriculum as having particular challenges. Assessing enterprise skills is not the same as assessing subject knowledge and exam/coursework skills that may occur within an individual lesson or across a course. In order for Enterprise Education to be successful and impactful, learning needs to be planned and assessed - with different sets of expectations for different ages.

Teamwork is a common focus for enterprise events. When learners are expected to identify how they exhibit teamwork or have developed teamworking skills, then the way that this is expressed should not be the same for a Year 7 learner as it is for a Year 12 learner. A Year 7 learner may be able to identify the different roles that individuals took in a team, and how the team could have worked better. For a Year 12 or Year 13 learner, I would be inclined to use a model such as Dr. Meredith Belbin's "Team Role Theory," so that they think more deeply about the roles that need to be fulfilled to ensure that a team works efficiently and effectively.

Progress in lessons is already recognised as a requisite for good teaching; this is equally true with regards to enterprise skills. However, assessing this may be difficult if enterprise is delivered as a large-scale event where there is limited time to be able to assess individual learners. In this situation, it is not only important to state learning outcomes but identifying success criteria is key, with opportunities for learners to be able to self-assess their learning against those success criteria at specific points within the event/day. It may be that differentiated success criteria are used so that learners can genuinely assess the quality of their enterprise skills. To take these further, learners may be required to engage in target setting for themselves, which would show evidence of reflecting on their learning with the intention to improve.

This approach of self-reflection and target setting can be used when assessing progress over time. Those schools that have a commitment to both Enterprise Education and employability often produce documentation that learners use throughout a year, or longer. An example of this is the Enterprise Passport, where learners record when, how, and to what extent they use enterprise skills - in individual lessons, in school organised events, and outside of school. This approach is one that has already been adopted in some Further Education (FE) and Higher Education (HE) institutions. The idea of a Digital Passport has also been proposed by employers whereby learners and employees can record evidence of their development of Enterprise skills across time and while studying at different educational establishments. It can be argued, therefore, that the use of an Enterprise Passport is an important one not only as a repository of evidence of Enterprise skills but is itself developing an important skill of creating an evidence base for a CV.

For the enterprise coordinator: what makes for successful Enterprise Education?

A school may have a commitment to Enterprise Education, either to expose learners to a range of educational experiences or with an explicit intention to improve learner enterprise skills and/or employability. In either case, in order to promote this the school leadership will give an individual member of staff the responsibility to develop this aspect of the school's curriculum, i.e. an enterprise coordinator.

The value of enterprise education within a school will be linked to the level of seniority of the enterprise coordinator. However, for many Business and Economics teachers who are beginning their career, becoming an enterprise coordinator has been an early step on the career ladder for them, with many going on to become department heads after this role. It allows learners to develop management skills as they will need to liaise and negotiate with other members of staff within the school. In addition, it can mean that opportunities are created whereby learners gain a positive view of the subject ahead of option choices in Year 9 or Year 11, as well as to develop key transferable skills for the future. Thus, being an enterprise coordinator can be a marketing and recruitment tool for your subject area, thereby improving the standing of both you and your department across the school.

As has been implied earlier, a key element is to develop an understanding of Enterprise Education that is shared by those colleagues who are delivering the enterprise programme and reflects both citizenship curriculum requirements together with employer expectations. A starting point would be to develop a list of knowledge, understanding, and skills that learners should be able to develop. I would argue that this should include business and economics understanding and financial capability, as well as soft skills such as teamwork and communication. By doing this, the list would reflect both the national curriculum and employer surveys. Also, communication could include the use of different media, including the way that businesses use Facebook, Twitter, Instagram, etc.

From this shared starting point of a specific set of enterprise knowledge, understanding, and skills, staff training could then ensure that all colleagues involved have sufficient expertise to deliver in these areas. This would then allow for the subsequent development of an Enterprise Education programme that would be accessible to all learners. In addition, the progress of learners would be assessed and tracked against the expectations of their knowledge, understanding, and skills as for any other programmes of study. Ideally, learners would be able to articulate how those skills are transferable between contexts, perhaps by undertaking follow-up discussions in form time.

Where such a clearly articulated programme of study exists then it would automatically follow that evaluations will be cognisant of the achievement of learning as well as enjoyment. Alongside the evaluation of learner achievement through the programme would be the regular review of employer expectations, which would be achieved by liaising with local employers, and perhaps working with the Head of Careers on this.

Reflection point:

1 What would you include in a list of Enterprise knowledge, understanding, and skills?
2 What would you consider to be the key success criteria for an Enterprise Day or event?
3 Choosing one of those items, what would you expect of a Year 8 learner? What would be different for a Year 11 learner?
4 How could you track learner progress across a year?

Financial literacy

As indicated above, in some definitions financial capability is a key aspect of Enterprise Education, a non-statutory subject. In contrast, financial literacy and personal finance are both statutory requirements and are contained within the National Curriculum (2014) at Key Stage 3 and Key stage 4 within Personal, Social, Health, and Economic education (PSHE) and the new GCSE Mathematics qualifications. In addition, at Key Stage 5, the Northern Council for Further Education (NCFE) is introducing a Level 3 Certificate in Mathematics for Everyday Life (from September 2019), which is focused on personal finance. Opportunities to develop both financial literacy and a knowledge and understanding of personal finance exist elsewhere within the Secondary curriculum.

Despite the introduction of the statutory requirement for financial literacy at Key Stage 3 and Key stage 4, financial education is considered to be ineffective, with one-third of teachers not knowing that it is on the curriculum and a majority indicating that the introduction of the requirement has made no difference to its delivery within their school (The Money Charity, 2016). There are a number of reasons for this: the lack of prioritisation, pressure for examination results, the lack of leadership, and the lack of expertise within schools, and where there is such expertise it is not being used effectively. Despite this, there are teachers who do believe that financial literacy and personal finance should be delivered by schools for the wider benefit of learners. Moreover, recommendations include that the delivery uses real-life examples and simulations, and that financial organisations do more to support financial literacy within schools and colleges. In order to address these issues, two aspects need to be considered: identifying what is required by the curriculum and where supporting materials can be found in order to ensure staff have the expertise to deliver the subject.

Curriculum requirements

Citizenship requires key stage 3 learners to be taught about: *"the functions and uses of money, the importance and practice of budgeting, and managing risk."* At key stage 4, learners are expected to be taught about: *"'income and expenditure, credit and debt, insurance, savings and pensions, financial products and services, and how public money is raised and spent."* Both of these requirements recognise that a key aim of Citizenship is to enable learners to take their place within society *"as responsible citizens, manage their money well, and make sound financial decisions."* [DfE National curriculum in England: Citizenship programmes of study for key stage 3 and key stage 4, (2014)]. However, the expectations of learners' engagement with the topics are different. At key stage 3, the emphasis is on personal finance and developing skills to manage their own money in the future. At key stage 4, the topics are to be addressed within the wider context of public policy and the inter-action between personal decision making and our roles as public citizens.

Traditional expectations of financial education are more likely to be found within Personal, Social, Health and Economic education (PSHE). Where this is delivered well, learners are equipped to manage their money in the future as well as in the present and the internal and external factors that influence our decision making are explored, e.g. attitude to risk, family commitments, impact on mental health and well-being, and career planning. These considerations have a clear overlap with the key stage 3 Citizenship curriculum, which can be reviewed and developed at key stage 4. It could be argued that this would need to be addressed again at key stage 5, although there is no statutory requirement to do so.

A stated purpose of the Mathematics National Curriculum is to provide learners with essential skills for life including that of financial literacy, as well as preparing them for employment. At key stage 3, it is to be used to "solve problems", and is identified specifically within "Ratio, proportion, and rates of change" linked to the ability to solve problems involving "simple interest in financial mathematics." At key stage 4, learners are expected to be able to apply their mathematical knowledge in financial contexts and, again, linked to the ability to solve problems. It is mentioned specifi-cally within algebra and the use of "graphs in financial contexts" for the more able learner. While the introduction of financial literacy within the Mathematics National Curriculum is welcomed, it is clear that the statutory requirements are less than for PSHE or Citizenship and materials from the exam boards lack any significant real-world contextualisation. In some quarters, concern has been raised at the quality of the way in which financial literacy is being addressed by the exam boards, and therefore, the teaching of the topic within GCSE Mathematics lessons.

The NCFE Level 3 Certificate in Mathematics for Everyday Life is designed for the post-16 learner and to support mathematics progression from key stage 4 as delivered in secondary school. The intention is to make the connection between mathematics and the demands of everyday life, including personal finance, commerce, chance, and the use of data. In my opinion, it is disappointing that the opportunity to develop budget-ing skills for this age group has been missed.

Supporting materials

The following list of organisations provides a flavour of what is available to schools to support the delivery of financial literacy within schools beyond the normal exam board support. The organisations take different approaches. Some provide free resources; for others, resources have to be paid for. Some provide consultants to support delivery; others provide resources to support the teachers in school. Most do not lead to qualifi-cations for students – but some do.

A key provider of financial education support and materials is **Young Money**, for-merly the Personal Finance Education Group (or pfeg), (www.young-money.org.uk), which merged with Young Enterprise in 2014. The materials, Continuing Professional Development (CPD), and events cover the whole of the financial literacy curriculum – including that of mathematics delivery – and across ALL key stages. It is recognised for the quality of its resources and support as well as the breadth of its expertise. Also, the majority of resources are free.

Another player in the field of delivering financial education is the **Money Charity** (www.themoneycharity.org.uk). Young Money recognises that the majority of financial education that will occur in schools will be by teachers, who are not experts, and so it provides support and materials to address this. The Money Charity takes a different approach, which is to use consultants to deliver financial education within schools. Resources are then developed for teachers to supplement the consultants' delivery. The website provides some very good resources in terms of advice and information, which are freely available to teachers.

Some banks and financial institutions have created resources for use in the classroom. An example is **MoneySense** which has been developed by the National Westminster Bank (https://natwest.mymoneysense.com/home) and includes a virtual bank, videos, and games, as well as a range of guides.

There are a number of games that have been written in response to the curriculum requirements, such as Keep The Cash (www.keepthecashgame.com), which is a one-day simulation whereby learners have to manage their own financial affairs as they would as adults. Another game is Bamzonia (https://bamzonia.com), which is delivered over a longer period of time. While these resources have good reviews, they can be expensive as well.

Some schools and colleges use the opportunity to develop student financial capability to enhance the CVs of their students by delivering this aspect of the curriculum through specific qualifications, such as those provided by the **London Institute of Banking & Finance (LIBF)**, which can be at Level 1, Level 2, and Level 3. The London Institute of Banking & Finance is also responsible for The Student Investor Challenge competition. For further information go to: http://www.libf.ac.uk/study/financial-capability/qualifications. **The Chartered Institute of Securities and Investments** (www.cisi.org) offers qualifications at Level 2 and Level 3 to develop learner understanding of securities and investment – and to provide an entry into the industry.

Embedding higher-order skills development within the "ordinary" Business or Economics lesson

Reflection point:

1 When you write a lesson plan for a topic that is new to your learners, where do you start?
2 How do you assess learning?
3 When do you assess learning?
4 Do you always control the lesson?

When we start teaching, we tend to see the assessment objectives of a qualification as being distinct from each other and needing to be addressed individually. In addition, the way in which lesson planning is introduced there is an equivalent emphasis on separate learning objectives, which are assessed sequentially. This allows learners and new teachers to develop strategies that scaffold learner's capability and understanding of what is required within the exam. However, there are other ways of enabling learners to develop deeper thinking that will enhance the development of transferable life skills. There are many approaches to developing higher-order thinking skills. the following are only examples of approaches that can be adopted.

Using student knowledge – not your own

Rather than using your own business knowledge, get learners to use their own business knowledge to deepen their understanding of key concepts. This may mean going outside of your comfort zone, but learners love being in control. It forces them to justify their decisions to both you and others in the class. For example, using the Boston Matrix, learners would have to justify their choice of music artist or group for each category. Their decisions would then be subject to peer review and then the class would have to agree which category the artist/group fitted into. This usually leads to some lively debate as learners must persuade both their peers and the teacher that their decisions are valid. Not only does this approach develop the learners' analytical and evaluative skills, but also their verbal communication skills.

Starting with the case study – not the (exam) questions

Many lessons use Bloom's Taxonomy to scaffold student learning. The case study is introduced at the *end* of the lesson to test learners' skills and understanding, particularly of analysis and evaluation. A different approach would be to introduce the case study *first* and ask learners to annotate the material, identifying information that provides insight into the business and explaining what this tells them about the business. It can also be an opportunity for them to identify aspects that require further clarification. This develops learner literacy skills by asking them to engage with the materials, as well as develop their business expertise. Group discussion can further develop their understanding as they share their insights into the passage. Moreover, the insights can be categorised on the board, perhaps in terms of opportunities and threats for the business. Thus student knowledge is being developed by introducing key terms to frame understanding on the back of their analysis (which is an evaluative skill). Questions can then start to be introduced to investigate management decision making based on the information within the case study.

Teaching without learning objectives

The task below has been used with different groups. For example, with A level students it was used to introduce equality legislation With student teachers, it was used to introduce fundamental British values. Within PSHE, it was used to investigate attitudes and stereotypes. If the learning objectives are introduced *before* the task is undertaken, the impact is lost and the learning is superficial. The task itself will develop learner skills of self-reflection, analysis, and evaluation in terms of their own attitudes and those of their peers, as well as provide the opportunity to consider the wider implications of those attitudes

The learners work in groups and once the task is completed, results are compared and considered. As the intergroup comparisons are made, the learners will be analysing and evaluating their own responses relative to those made by other groups. As the teacher, you can guide the learners to assess the influences that have led them to their own choices and the wider impact of those choices. Some will seek to justify their attitudes and their use of stereotypes, which are *always* evident. Others will see that they need to identify the wider context and impact of their decision making, and maybe even to revise their viewpoints. With skillful direction, the teacher can challenge choices along ethical, moral, and legislative lines. How you guide the subsequent discussion will depend on your overarching learning objective for the lesson. The end of the task and/ or lesson will expect learners to decide what the learning objectives have been, and to what extent they have been achieved.

TASK: West Street

You are part of the writing team for a new soap opera called *West Street*. There are five characters that you want to introduce: Police officer, Nurse, Shop assistant, Bank manager, Painter and decorator

The writing team need to discuss and define the characterisation of these five people.

Using the list below in Figure 7.1, choose three words that will help to describe the characters. Identify two other characteristics not included in the list.

Once this has been done, choose names for each of the characters.

The decisions that can be made are made by the writing team can be inputted into the table below in Figure 7.2

Pretty	Handsome	Clumsy	Ordinary
Honest	Ambitious	Happy	Manipulative
Macho	Caring	Spiteful	Opportunist
Aggressive	Scatterbrained	Organised	Passive
Kind	Enthusiastic	Suffering from OCD	Motivated
Violent	Disorganised	Assertive	Optimist
Dyslexic	Smart	Pessimist	Flirtatious
Naïve	Scheming	Time wasting	Busy body
Self-satisfied	Determined	Adventurous	Two-timing

Figure 7.1 List of characteristics for use with *West Street*.

Character	Police officer	Nurse	Shop assistant	Bank manager	Painter and decorator
Characteristics (3 from the list)					
2 more characteristics					
Name					

Figure 7.2 Descriptions of *West Street* characters.

Learner well-being

The emphasis within this chapter has been on developing wider skills of learners that easily come within the remit of the subject area, i.e. employability skills, enterprise, financial capability, and higher-order thinking. Within the current climate of increasing mental health issues that learners face, it seems fitting to raise some awareness of the impact that Business and Economics teachers can have on the well-being for their learners. It is worth noting that teachers are identified as the first tier of mental health support for young people. This does not mean that we are expected to be experts in the field, but we need to know that we have a responsibility to support learner well-being, to be able to recognise symptoms, and to report our concerns. This section fails to do justice to this huge area. There should be support for staff within schools. At the end of this section is a list of websites that can provide further information.

It is regularly the case that when visiting schools the Business and Economics teachers will indicate that the behaviour of learners is often better than elsewhere in the school. This is particularly evident with those learners who have a reputation for being challenging. The behaviour of learners within the classroom is a clear indicator of how they feel not only about the subject but also about their teacher and the environment within which they are studying. The implication is that learners are more likely to feel secure when studying Business or Economics. This evidence is only anecdotal and here is no research that identifies why this might be the case. The following information is put forward as suggestions based upon discussions with school-based staff.

Business and Economics are not core subjects. While this has negative impact in terms of subject security and finance for the teaching staff, it can mean that there is less direct pressure on students to achieve within these subjects. This does not mean that there is *no* imperative for our learners to do well - or to meet their target grades - but that we have the freedom to manage this differently and with more creativity than core subjects. A straightforward example of this was in the writing of end-of-term reports for key stage 4 learners. Instead of using the formulaic wording of '"making good/excellent progress against … targets" the statement "You are rising like a phoenix" was used. This captured the imagination of the students and was arguably more motivational than any formula. With key stage 5 learners, enabling them to write and address targets that are developed collaboratively with teaching staff, and using data as one source of information, can be a powerful tool in developing learner agency and giving them a sense of empowerment.

Good Business and Economics teaching is rooted in current events - bringing in local news stories, businesses, and politics as well as national and international news stories. Therefore, learners are taught to make links between what they are learning and their everyday lives. For those learners who are not well-supported at home in terms of their education, being able to see the relevance of their learning to their life outside of school is very important, not least of which because it helps them to make sense of the world that they live in.

Moreover, Business is a very broad subject. This means that there is usually some aspect that learners will do well in - and which good teachers will recognise and reward. This may not always be in terms of academic achievement, but in the way you develop the subject and give them opportunities to excel. For example, when teaching a law unit we staged a mock courtroom experience. I cannot say that it was particularly realistic, but it did give some previously quiet and disengaged students the opportunity to perform and show a much better understanding of legal concepts than anticipated. If someone is good at managing other members of the class, encourage them to be a group leader on a regular basis. Make sure that their developing management skills are related back to their form tutor and appear on reports and references.

In my discussions, the theme of developing approaches to rewarding good behaviour regularly arose. Sometimes, this would be in using a tick system on the board (rather than the traditional tick system for poor behaviour). Other school reward systems include sending postcards home or telephone calls at the end of the week. A key feature was prioritising the rewarding of good behaviour of those learners with a poor reputation elsewhere in the school.

In order for our learners to be successful they need to feel secure and valued (which is also true for staff). While we may have little influence in terms of external factors that affect our learners, we do have all the influence we need in order to provide them with an environment where they are respected by their teacher and their fellow learners, and supported to achieve their best, whatever that is.

As indicated at the start, mental well-being of learners is a growing area of significance for the teacher and there is a lot of external support available. There is a short list of websites at the end of the chapter to enable you to pursue this further.

Conclusion

The intention of this chapter has been to deepen your concept of teaching Business – to include the development of a wider skills set than may have been the case at the start of your teaching career. I have tried to provide a wide range of considerations for you to analyse and evaluate. There are no right answers about how to develop the teaching of your subject in your context. What is important is for you to keep questioning, and to keep improving and enhancing your understanding of what it means to "inspire, motivate, and challenge" yourself and your learners. Chapter 9 "The Reflective Practitioner: the place of reflection in the continuous development of programmes and practitioners" will develop this theme further.

References

Bamzonia Personal Financial Education (online) (2019).) Available from: www.v2.bamzonia.com [Accessed 23 January 2019]

Chartered Institute for Securities and Investments (online) (2019). Available from: www.cisi.org.uk [Accessed 23 January 2019]

Department for Education (2014). National curriculum in England: mathematics programmes of study. Gov.UK (online). Available from: https://www.gov.uk/government/publications/national-curriculum-in-england-mathematics-programmes-of-study [Accessed 23 January 2019]

Department for Education (2013). National curriculum in England: citizenship programmes of study. Gov.UK (online). Available from: https://www.gov.uk/government/publications/national-curriculum-in-england-citizenship-programmes-of-study [Accessed 23 January 2019]

ICAEW.com. The Institute of Chartered Accountants in England and Wales (2018). BASE competition (online). Available from: http://careers.icaew.com/campaigns/base-competition [Accessed 23 January 2019]

Knapton, Helena (2014). "Developing Business Links," *Teaching Business & Economics* October, 18 (3): 20–22.

KTC Financial Skills for Real Life (2019). Keep The Cash (online). Available from: www.keepthecashgame.com [Accessed 23 January 2019]

Lord Young (2014). *Enterprise for All: The Relevance of Enterprise in Education*,' London: Crown Copyright.

My Kinda Future (2019). MyKindaFuture (online). Available from: https://www.mykindafuture.com/Educator [Accessed 23 January 2019]

NatWest (2019). MoneySense: Making Sense of Money (online). Available from: https://natwest.mymoneysense.com/home [Accessed 23 January 2019]

Ofsted (2011). Economics, Business and Enterprise Education. Manchester: Crown Copyright (online). Available from: https://www.gov.uk/government/publications/economics-business-and-enterprise-education [Accessed 23 January 2019]

Ofsted (2016). Getting Ready for Work. Manchester: Crown Copyright (online). Available from: https://www.gov.uk/government/publications/enterprise-education-how-secondary-schools-prepare-young-people-for-work [Accessed 23 January 2019]

Teach a Man to Fish (2018). The School Enterprise Challenge (online). Available from: http://www.schoolenterprisechallenge.org/about/about-us [Accessed 23 January 2019]

The London Institute of Banking & Finance (2018). Student Investor Challenge (online). Available from: http://www.studentinvestor.org [Accessed 23 January 2019]

The London Institute of Banking & Finance (2019). Financial Qualifications (online). Available from: http://www.libf.ac.uk/study/financial-capability/qualifications [Accessed 23 January 2019]

The Money Charity (online) (2019). Available from: www.themoneycharity.org.uk [Accessed 23 January 2019]

Young Enterprise (2018). *The Tenner Challenge Young Enterprise* (online). Available from: https://www.young-enterprise.org.uk/what-we-do/secondary-programmes/tenner [Accessed 23 January 2019]

Young Enterprise (2019). *Young Money* (online). Available from: www.young-money.org.uk [Accessed 23 January 2019]

Further reading (mental health)

Beat (2019). Beat Eating Disorders (online). Available from: https://www.b-eat.co.uk [Accessed 23 January 2019]

Chasing the Stigma (2018). Normalising & Humanising Mental Illness (online). Available from: https://chasingthestigma.co.uk [Accessed 23 January 2019]

Chasing the Stigma (2019). Hub of Hope (online). Available from: https://hubofhope.co.uk/services [Accessed 23 January 2019]

Family Lives (2019). Bullying UK (online) Available from: http://www.familylives.org.uk [Accessed 23 January 2019]

Harmless (2019). Self-harm doesn't discriminate…(online) Available from: http://www.harmless.org.uk [Accessed 23 January 2019]

MHFA England (2019). Mental Health First Aid (online). Available from: https://mhfaengland.org [Accessed 23 January 2019]

The Children's Society (2018). Understanding Adolescent Neglect Troubled Teens (online). Available from: https://www.childrenssociety.org.uk/what-we-do/research/troubled-teens-understanding-adolescent-neglect [Accessed 23 January 2019]

Young Minds (2018). Young Minds Fighting for Young People's Mental Health Impact Report, 2017–18 (online). Available from: https://youngminds.org.uk/media/2701/impact-report-2018.pdf [Accessed 23 January 2019]

Young Minds (2019). Young Minds' Blog (online). Available from: https://youngminds.org.uk/blog [Accessed 23 January 2019]

8

MAXIMISING THE USE OF RESOURCES

- Introduction – resource challenges
- Finances – how to spend your budget wisely; how to increase your funds
- Human resources – working with individuals you have easy access to but are not members of the department
- Professional networks
- Digital resources
- Non-technical resources
- Trips
- Research
- Conclusion

Introduction – resource challenges

Towards the end of the Postgraduate Certificate in Education (PGCE) programme I was leading we had an event whereby student teachers collaborated in small groups, each with a Head of Business and/or Economics from a partnership school and working on a departmental problem linked to the A level specification, i.e. budgetary strategy and control. Although the simulation was linked to an A level specification, the invited Heads of Department (HoD) included one HoD whose department only delivered vocational qualifications. In addition to the HoDs, we had an ex-Maths teacher who had moved into industry and was then working with schools on how to use their budgets better. By working with her employer, the Crown Commissioning Service (CCS), the schools were able to buy in bulk and at strategic times of the year. The learning intention for the PGCE learners had been to show how a business simulation could be used to develop A level student skills of analysis and evaluation, thereby linking exam skills with the real world. The learning intention for the day was fully met and it was great to see the PGCE student teachers identify that there were other ways of developing A level skills that were not just about writing answers to A level questions. However, what was more interesting to me was the discussion that developed between the different groups and their HoDs as they heard how others managed their budgets or *increased* their budgets. It became transparent that the issue of managing budgets was one they had received no training for, that HoDs meetings in school would not address, and that some of the lessons they learned were ones they felt that they should have thought of as Business and Economics specialists. The HoDs recognised the experience was transferable into their own context, both as a pedagogical approach and in their role as HoD. As they left, some of the HoDs felt it was one of their best Continuing Professional Development (CPD) experiences, even though they were there to support the delivery of the PGCE.

As you will have recognised, the development of this business simulation was against a backdrop of significant challenge to both Business and Economics teachers. In recent years, we have seen huge changes in the curriculum being offered in secondary schools. As identified in earlier chapters, the argument for these radical changes has been the government's intention to ensure that all learners from all backgrounds have equality of opportunity. Consequently, the emphasis is on the core (Maths and English) and "facilitating subjects." The term facilitating subjects is one that was developed by the Russell Group of universities as being subjects that these universities consider to be most likely to allow applicants to gain entry into their courses. These subjects have found their way into what has been termed the English Baccalaureate (EBacc) and are represented in Progress 8 measures. Business and Economics are not specifically represented in this list of subjects, and so schools and teachers of these subjects are under pressure to ensure that their place is maintained within the curriculum as many schools are limiting the range of choice to their learners.

Moreover, the press is regularly reporting the challenges that schools are facing in terms of funding, despite the government's position that more is being spent on education. Where schools are still committed to the delivery of Business, Economics, and Enterprise, the school leadership is faced with difficult decisions. As a result, subjects such as Business and Economics, vocational qualifications such as BTEC or the Cambridge Technical, and wider school experiences such as Enterprise Education have lost out in terms of both curriculum time and financial support. This chapter has been included because of the Business simulation experience written against a challenging education and school backdrop. The examples that I use, like elsewhere in the book, come as a result of working with colleagues in different settings, where they are able to make their resources go further and enable their learners to get better and broader experiences as a result. As with everything else in the book, there will be parts you will want to adopt immediately and there will be others that will be for the longer term. There will be those that become your favourites and those that you will never touch. You are the expert of your own needs, your own learners, and your own internal drivers. So, as elsewhere, the way you use this information is your choice.

Reflection point:

What do you consider to be your main challenges as a Business or Economics teacher as you develop your subject?

- Your learners?
- Ensuring you have sufficient curriculum time?
- Making the best use of your budget?
- Engaging the learners with the subject?
- Providing a wider perspective?

While this chapter includes suggestions for a range of resources, it will overlap and be complementary to other parts of this book. For example, Chapter 6 "Learning and teaching strategies: Differentiation" includes approaches to differentiation that are easy to implement and are transferable across groups. Chapter 7 "Developing wider skills: seeing beyond the specification" includes a section that is about capacity building within the department.

Finances – how to spend your budget wisely; how to increase your funds

This chapter began with the Business simulation around the theme of strategic budgetary control and so we will begin with the lessons learnt on that day. The employer that we were working with was the Crown Commissioning Service (CCS). This is a government organisation and one of its roles is to provide an aggregation service. This is where public sector organisations, such as schools, can tap into their bulk-buying power to reduce the cost of purchases to themselves. Not only this, but the CCS tracks the costs of their purchases and potential purchases throughout the year so that they can identify those periods when products are at their most expensive and when they are at their cheapest. What was apparent from the Business simulation was that HoDs tended to do their largest purchases either at the end of the summer term or at the start of the autumn term, when the costs of school goods – pens, paper, and textbooks – are at their highest. By working with the data the CCS provided, the HoDs realised that they could make much better use of their limited budgets by making their purchases at other times of the year when the costs would be lower. Moreover, even greater savings could be made by working with the CCS to make their purchases. At the time of writing the CCS website says "95 schools saved an average of 36 percent on 2,200 tablets". While you may be wanting to make much more mundane purchases, an online inquiry is still worth pursuing at: https://www.gov.uk/guidance/ccs-aggregation.

Using the CCS is a way of enabling the department to save money. With some of the HoDs it became apparent that they were also adept at raising funds – for learners and for the department. In Chapter 7 "developing wider skills: seeing beyond the specification," there is a section on using competitions as a way of engaging with Business in order to broaden the experience of learners and to develop their wider life and employability skills, which should be the main driver for engaging learners in such competitions. Examples of the competitions within that chapter are BASE, the ICAEW's National Business and Accounting competition (http://careers.icaew.com/campaigns/base-competition), and the Student Investor Challenge (http://www.studentinvestor.org) which is run by The London Institute of Banking & Finance. As with any competition, the winners are rewarded with prizes. With a number of these competitions, the reward is financial together with opportunities to gain wider business experiences. Moreover, organisations appear to be widening their policy in terms of rewards with winners at different levels of the competition and so participation is being rewarded as well as final success. In a few cases, it appears that HoDs are able to negotiate with their learners so that any financial rewards are shared with the department and are not just kept by the learners themselves. This obviously requires some skill, which may include a discussion about how the funds could be spent for the benefit of the learners within the subject area, and may need some wider negotiation with the hierarchy of the school.

Another approach that is used regularly is the use of enterprise activities. One example is the department that runs a stationery shop within the school. Learners manage the stationery shop, which is seen by the school as an opportunity for learners (not just those studying Business) to develop their skills and confidence in addition to an awareness of how businesses work. The profits of the shop are then used to enhance the departmental budget. Other approaches include the use of standalone events, such as Enterprise Days or during parents' evenings, where learners run a small-scale business and the profits are shared between the learners and the department.

Where there is a competitive element to learning, then rewards need not come out of the departmental budget. I had a colleague whose background was in the brewery industry and it was a constant source of surprise to colleagues at how the opportunity to win a bar towel motivated learners. While this may not be something that you have or want to share, you will find that a number of businesses are prepared to provide some element of gift at the end of the school year. For example, cinema vouchers or meal vouchers have been regularly sourced for such events.

Where trips are being undertaken, the timing of these excursions need also be considered. Most of the time, there will be the need for the trip to link specifically to a module or topic as it is being taught. However, this may not always be the case, particularly with a two-year course. Where possible, trips should be timed to occur *after* the summer exams. This is a time when student numbers in the school/college are at their lowest and, therefore, the costs of class cover can be reduced significantly. If a trip can be planned to be local, so that the length of the trip is limited to one-half day or less, then the trip costs are further lowered.

A less common source of finance was where a HoD reported that he/she had been able to set up a discrete fund for the business department, which had been created using money provided by an ex-student of the school. While this was a result of the ex-student's initiative, rather than the HoD, working with previous learners is an aspect that may be worth pursuing, i.e. tapping into the alumni. This is an approach that is widely used by Higher Education and the private education sector, although this is usually for the benefit of the *entire* institution rather than a single department.

Another source of finance to be considered is that of research grants or charitable funding. Accessing such funds usually requires support from the school leadership, although the impetus will come from key members of staff. In the current climate, most funding is used to support those from disadvantaged backgrounds and/or the disengaged with poor life chances; the funding is often linked to arts projects or addressing specific skills, such as managing conflict. While this approach is more specialised it is one worth considering, particularly if it means working with another department to enlarge the educational experience of learners. The Education Endowment Foundation (https://educationendowmentfoundation.org.uk) is one charity that actively looks for school-based research projects to support the disadvantaged.

Human resources – working with individuals you have easy access to but are not members of the department

In Chapter 7 "Developing wider skills: seeing beyond the specification," there is a short section on how to develop the capacity of the department in terms of enabling learners to engage with business more widely. Capacity is often an issue, particularly within a school setting where the Business department may be particularly small and where class sizes may be relatively large. This section will develop this theme of how to enhance the human resources capacity of the department.

Working with learners has already been touched upon within this chapter in order to increase the funding of the department. While working with learners is not necessarily the first port of call when developing the department, it can be one that is very effective. Working with learners on enterprise events or stationery stalls or competitions all improve the reputation of the department – and of the school. On the one hand, this is because of the positive impact on learners' personal development. On the other hand, there is the wider contribution to the school ethos and, therefore, to the school's reputation in the community. However, providing these wider experiences may increase the demands on your time rather than a way of building capacity.

There are other ways in which creating opportunities for learners to work with you can be applied more widely and will enable you to build the capacity of the department. Academic buddy systems, which may be called "student academic mentors" or "peer mentors", is an approach to teaching and learning that is gaining wide acceptance as a way of providing learners with increased responsibility and developing learner communication and negotiating skills (which can be added to their curriculum vitae), with the added advantage of providing additional support and guidance for those learners who need it. This can be developed by having Year 13 learners work with Year 12 learners, or even with Year 11 learners. While it will require some additional training for the student mentors in the short term, there will be medium and long-term benefits for staff. This is particularly true for those staff working within a school or college where they are expected to provide out-of-lesson intervention.

With both initiatives – enterprise enhancements and the academic buddy system – learners' enhance the working of the department from within the school. In addition, learners can increase engagement beyond the school gates by providing teaching staff with access to individuals outside of school through their own networks. In some cases, these contacts will be a way in which learners can improve their understanding of concepts covered in class by the careful framing of homework tasks such as research, which may include the requirement to work in small groups in order to write appropriate questions and interview individuals. Investigating perceptions of the impact of leaving the European Union (EU) would be an interesting question to investigate at this time and would it would feed into both the Economics and Business curricula. Alternatively, you can ask learners to make suggestions as to who may be useful to invite to speak to the class about their business. Often this requires some prompting, as learners will need to be guided on who they know that would be available to speak to the class.

Being able to network is a much-needed skill within the modern working world, and teaching is no different. This includes networking within the school and identifying ways in which synergies can be developed across subjects. This may include identifying ways in which you can piggyback activities that are planned either for the school or for other subjects. An example of this is work experience that many schools still deliver. In these instances, setting tasks for your learners that link the work experience with the specification that is being delivered is a useful enhancement to their learning. Many schools use visits to theme parks as a reward as well as opportunities for extending their learning. Many theme parks – and other large visitor destinations – have education centres that will arrange talks and provide resources linked to particular aspects of the curriculum and qualifications. By making these connections, the time involved in planning the trip is reduced significantly and improves the quality of the experience for your learners. In addition, because the trip is arranged across subjects the impact on teaching at school is reduced and, therefore, the amount of cover needed will also be reduced.

Opportunities to work across departments in other ways can be developed in order to enhance the reputation of the department. For example, working with the Languages department can lead to activities that improve understanding of international business and working across cultures. Working with the RE department on trade can improve student understanding of the implications of their purchasing decisions on the lives of people making their goods. An excellent example of this is the Trading Trainers game by Christian Aid (https://www.christianaid.org.uk/sites/default/files/2017-08/trading-trainers-game.pdf).

Another way of networking within the school is by recognising that the school is not only a business in its own right; the school has businesses that operate within it. One common example of this is the canteen, which is usually outsourced. An excellent lesson I observed was where the teacher had previously prepared a lesson with the manager of the canteen within a series of three lessons focusing on quality control. It was the midpoint in these lessons and with a group of learners who had the reputation for being disengaged and unable to achieve much. During the previous lesson, learners had developed questions to put to the canteen manager. The opening questions that learners developed were quite broad in order to enable them to have a good understanding of the different aspects of running a canteen. The later questions then became focused on managing quality control within the canteen. The canteen manager had been provided beforehand with a list of the questions so that she could prepare her answers. The interview of the canteen manager was combined with a tour of the canteen. This allowed both the canteen manager and learners the opportunity to become relaxed with each other before engaging in the specific aspect of the interview. Following the interview, learners were allowed time to discuss the answers to ensure that they each had a common understanding of what had been said in response to their questions. During the following lesson, the answers were written up. It is worth noting that a week later the class was observed by a senior member of staff whose feedback included a comment which indicated that he hadn't realised that these learners were capable of as much as they were doing or able to be as engaged.

Another way of developing the capacity of the department in terms of human resources comes from working with those who are training to become teachers. The incentives for schools to be involved in the delivery of teacher training have increased in recent years, including the introduction of the Apprenticeship Levy on employers and the apprenticeship route into teaching. If your school, or cluster of schools (if you are working within an Academy chain or school alliance), is involved in teacher training, then the department can benefit by working with them. This is easiest to organise if they are business trainees, when roles can be allocated to them from within the department. However, it is also the case that all student teachers, as well as established teachers, are expected to evidence ways in which they uphold the ethos of the school. Working with the Business/Economics department is one way that staff can evidence that they are doing this, particularly when working on particular events such as an Enterprise Day.

Another way of developing the capacity of a department is by working with local businesses. Corporate Social Responsibility (CSR) continues to be an area many businesses want to exploit as a way of improving or developing their brand, particularly within the local area. It is known that in some instances businesses want to use engagement with schools and colleges as a way of recruiting staff for the future. The introduction of the Apprenticeship Levy is expected to increase engagement with the apprenticeship agenda of government and result in an increased number of opportunities for young people to engage with this approach to career development. In turn, this may lead to increased competition amongst employers to recruit staff straight from school.

Historically, there are two challenges to overcome when teachers want to work with businesses. The first challenge is that many teachers believe that generating links with business is time-consuming. However, those schools and departments that do work with employers recognise that this is not necessarily the case. Large businesses will have local employees responsible for developing links with schools and colleges. In addition, the local Chamber of Commerce is often very helpful in brokering links between education and local businesses.

The second and more difficult challenge is to ensure that the link with the business is effective. This element can be time-consuming and businesses often struggle to manage the demands of fitting into a school timetable. To address this can take some ingenuity, such as using video links and constructing effective sets of questions that learners can ask. However, the benefits to learners' personal development are clear in terms of raising their aspirations, as well as addressing aspects of the curriculum.

Professional networks

It can be argued that working with professional associations, the main networks for the subject area, is another form of networking, or working with human resources, and may not be a way that you thought of in terms of "maximising resources." Firstly, the networks identified so far are not subject specific networks. This means that they are unlikely to be committed to your development, either in terms of your broader subject knowledge and pedagogy or in terms of your knowledge and understanding of the qualifications that are being developed. Secondly, making the most of the resources available to you is not just a case of providing materials to help you deliver the subject matter or about the department, but is also about your wider professional role. What is being addressed in this part of the chapter are those formal, and semi-formal subject-based networks that exist for the benefit of members' professional development. This can lead into career development, sometimes with exam boards, or by identifying and preparing for opportunities that exist within and between schools. This section identifies a selection of the subject-specific networks that exist, recognising there will be others as well. There are three main types of networks:

- Networks that exist to support the profession in broad terms.
- Networks that support specific subject development and delivery.
- Networks that are linked to specific qualifications.

An important professional association is the **Economics, Business and Enterprise Association (EBEA).** The strength and unique value of this professional association is in its role as advocate for the subject and its place within the curriculum to external stakeholders, such as the Department for Education (DfE) and Ofsted. When the curriculum for financial capability was being reviewed, key staff at the EBEA were able to coordinate a community response to the materials that were being developed. Ofsted has always been supportive of EBEA and subject inspectors look to see evidence of engagement with the wider business and economics teaching community, such as through membership in EBEA. Subject knowledge and pedagogical support for the subject community comes predominantly through the publication of its journal and newsletter, plus the provision of access to support materials on its website (https://ebea.org.uk). There are occasional webinars that have been well-received by those who have engaged with them. As is the case with most professional associations, membership is not free. However, there are various levels of membership, including corporate membership, whereby all members of the department are covered and which some schools/colleges are willing to fund.

Tutor2u (https://www.tutor2u.net) describe themselves as the Exam Performance Specialists and provide teachers with access to a broad range of qualification-related support. While having started out as providing support materials for those delivering the AQA A levels in Business and Economics, this organisation has grown substantially and continues to develop. The support provided ranges from materials that can be accessed both digitally and as hard copy, CPD events for teaching staff as well as large-scale revision sessions for learners. Social media is used extensively, such as the closed groups on Facebook, e.g. the BTEC Business Teachers Group and the AQA A Level Business Teachers. Key staff also use Twitter to promote current news stories to support subject delivery. A relatively recent development has been the introduction of a jobs board - both for teaching positions and exam boards, and for tutor2u.

Interest and engagement in **local teaching networks** appears to have been rediscovered in recent years and can be significant in terms of professional development. The development of Academy chains, teaching school clusters, and other affiliations between schools has led to increased collaboration and professional support within the local business and economics teaching community. In successful networks, there are opportunities to discuss and address changes in the wider educational context, such as the introduction of Progress 8. This is in addition to being able to address specific approaches to teaching and learning, from the simple approaches such as writing frames, to the more profound such as metacognitive approaches to teaching and learning. An important aspect of these groups is the emotional support that can be engendered together with practical responses to their teaching context.

Other networks also exist, such as the **Enterprise Village** (https://www.achievementbuilder.co.uk) which provides the opportunity to network through its Enterprise Register. Through the Register individuals are linked with schools in their area or with schools with specific areas of expertise. The Enterprise Village annual conference is well supported and draws in teachers, enterprise providers - national and local - and teacher-training providers. A developing network is a Teacher Advisory Group that is being managed by **Young Money** (www.young-money.org.uk) with the aim of ensuring that their information and materials are relevant to young people.

As well as providing online support materials and CPD opportunities, **exam boards** often promote the development of local networks that are focused on the delivery of particular qualifications. It means that issues can be dealt with quickly. Moreover, they allow the exam boards to address some common issues with a number of schools at one time. An added aspect of such networks is that career opportunities can arise for teachers to work with the exam boards and forms one of the exam board's approaches to recruitment. For teachers, working either as examiners or assessors generates a wider network for teachers when they communicate with staff from other schools. This is in addition to acquiring considerable insight into the expectations of the qualification that will feed into their teaching. For the teacher new to the demands of marking for the exam board there is an induction period which means that the number of scripts that are expected to be marked is normally capped.

The Chartered College of Teaching (https://chartered.college) has been described as the opportunity to re-professionalise teaching. A key element of this is through its Chartered Teacher programme. This certified professional development programme aims to develop and maintain excellence in teaching. In addition, it has a recognised network across the profession and therefore can represent the profession to external stakeholders, which other networks may not be able to do.

Both the **TES**, formerly known as the Times Education Supplement (www.tes.com) and **The Guardian** (www.theguardian.com/teacher-network) promote networks or communities within the teaching profession, where questions can be asked and addressed. The websites for these publications provide access to a wide range of lesson-specific materials and teaching vacancies, which complement the materials available on other websites. These websites also provide critical analysis of current research, education policy, and "fashions" in teaching and learning, which encourage you to take ownership of your professional identity.

Another online networking body that is increasing in its reach is **LinkedIn** (www.linkedin.com). A simple description of LinkedIn is that it is a networking site for a wide range of professionals. In the first instance, it provides access to a much wider body of teachers, including those who teach in international schools. LinkedIn has proved valuable in terms of obtaining other perspectives of teaching and learning, and opportunities for teaching overseas. As the aim of LinkedIn is to provide a forum for professionals, it enables teachers to connect with staff in other industries, which provides further insight into Business, as well as seeing the transferability of your skills to possible careers.

Reflection point:

1   Who would you identify as the people that support your development – as a teacher, as a Business/Economics teacher, or as an educator?
2   How do you want to develop as a teacher – in the short, medium, and long term?
3   Who will help you to achieve this?
4   What are the values that underpin your teaching?

Digital resources

Technology enhanced learning (TEL) is a phrase that is heard throughout education, with much energy invested in developing virtual learning environments (VLEs), which often become repositories of information rather than genuine learning environments. Developing TEL is a subject that is beyond the scope of this chapter – or this book – but I would encourage an approach that is critically inquisitive regarding what is available and can be used to genuinely enhance student learning. Many teachers use presentation software, such as available with Prezi (www.prezi.com) and Issuu (www.issuu.com), and online quizzes and games, such as Kahoot! (www.kahoot.com) and Socrative (www.socrative.com), as well as blogs and wikis to make their materials, lessons, and assessment more engaging. This is important, but must always be critiqued against the criterion: How does this deliver better learning? Peter Atherton's *50 ways to use technology enhanced learning in the classroom: practical strategies for teaching* (2018) is a useful book to have, as he makes genuine connections between learning and the technology.

An underused resource is often the exam boards themselves. They provide a wide range of resources: specifications, past papers online, schemes of work, subject specific materials, etc. The specifications and resources will give guidance on what they think a good course looks like and what they want learners to achieve through studying that course. Exam boards employ subject leads who provide personalised support and advice on request. For many Heads of Department (HoD), this is one of the factors that they take into account when choosing which exam board to work with. The following provide links to the main exam boards used for both Business and Economics:

- AQA (www.aqa.org.uk)
- OCR (www.ocr.org.uk)
- Eduqas (https://www.eduqas.co.uk)
- Pearson (https://qualifications.pearson.com/en/subjects/business.html)
- WJEC (www.wjec.co.uk)
- Cambridge International Organisation (www.cambridgeinternational.org), which offers the Cambridge Pre-U qualifications.

There are other organisations that provide online resources for teachers and learners that are not so closely aligned to specific exam boards. But they may be useful alternative sources of material and approaches in some circumstances. Please note that technology is always developing and so approaches become dated. Some examples include:

- TES (www.tes.com)
- Bee Business Bee (www.youtube.com/user/beebusinessbee)
- S-cool (www.s-cool.co.uk/a-level/business-studies)
- BusinessEd Supporting Business Education (www.businessed.co.uk/index.php/home/links)

There are a huge number of online videos on specific subject topics, such as price elasticity, Gross Domestic Product (GDP), etc. These have their place within lessons and for learners to access when revising. Using these videos when you feel that your subject knowledge is less than secure can be tempting, but there are significant risks to this. One is that the rest of the lesson is still in your hands and if you don't have a secure understanding, then leaving the explanation to someone else, i.e. the person on the video, can still be confusing to your learners. Sometimes the videos are wrong, or for a different audience. For example, using a video that is by an American and for an American audience can mean the subject terminology does not match that used in England. Sometimes, the choice of video expresses your lack of understanding rather than providing clarification, e.g. "aggregate demand" is a *macro*economic term, whereas "demand" is a *micro*economic term and its explanation is different.

Both Business and Economics are described as live subjects. This means they should be rooted in the world as it is experienced in the here and now. For this reason, it is considered to be good practice to encourage learners to follow business and economics news through different news organisations and business or economics reportage on Twitter or Facebook. Doing this yourself will ensure your own subject knowledge currency, and show your enthusiasm for the subject to your learners. Some examples include:

- Bloomberg (www.bloomberg.com/europe)
- The Economist (www.economist.com)
- BBC (www.bbc.co.uk)
- The Financial Times (www.ft.com)
- The Guardian (www.theguardian.com)
- BBC The World of Business Podcasts (https://www.bbc.co.uk/programmes/p02nrwfk)

A way of ensuring the availability of appropriate news stories to learners is by the use of an online a curation service such as Scoop it (www.scoop.it) to pull your stories together. Not only does this allow for the stories to be brought together, but it allows you to add commentary so that you can make those links to the curriculum. By doing this, learners will be able to see the "big picture" of the subject as well as provide up-to-date examples of individual topics.

Turning news stories into case studies is a way of enabling your learners to apply the subject knowledge developed in lessons. If this approach is too time-consuming for you to develop your own case studies, then Business Case Studies (http://businesscasestudies.co.uk) can be a cheap source of obtaining additional materials that are appropriate for A level. A note of caution - with Business Case Studies, there is a bias towards AQA, reflecting AQA's dominance in the A level Business market.

Non-technical resources

One of the characteristics of new teachers is the constant development and photocopying of handouts, including individual writing frames for pieces of work and differentiated worksheets. New teachers have a steep learning curve to identify and respond to learner needs. The development of individualised support for learners is one stage of the learning curve. The difficulty of this is compounded by having to move placements and adapt to another set of learners, which means a different set of differentiated work needs to be written to show that the student teacher can adapt to a new environment. Although these are necessary steps in a teacher's development, once a new teacher is in post there is a period of adaptation that should allow staff to become more efficient in the development and use of resources – both in terms of the materials produced and in the use of time.

It is one of the joys of starting your first teaching post that you can get to know and understand your learners to a greater degree than during teaching practice. Alongside this is the opportunity to create resources that can be used flexibly. It is an important step towards creating a work-life balance. As indicated in earlier chapters, an example is the creation of writing frames for different types of questions or styles of writing, which are then laminated. For example, whenever the learners are doing a 6 mark question then the writing frame for 6 mark questions is used. This can then be subject to increased sophistication by creating a range of writing frames for 6 mark questions that are differentiated according to the progress the learners are making. The intention is that no learners require a writing frame at all by the time they come to sit for the exam. It is a case of recognising that scaffolding needs to be taken away as well as put up – just as when building a house. Not only will this save time in the medium and long run, but it will also reduce the photocopying bill!

A number of teachers become adept at being able to adapt materials and approaches from outside of the classroom. Examples include:

- The use of a pack of cards to teach probability as an introduction to decision trees.
- Using the concept of the memory game where the player has to match images from a set of cards that are face down. Instead of images, the key term and the definition could be the matching pair so that both need to be collected to win that trick. I used this when delivering financial ratios, and learners were able to pick up the definitions quickly, which led to much more effective analysis of financial data than with previous cohorts of students.
- Spreadsheets can be used to set up stock exchange games. The document can be set up so that team members all have online and simultaneous access to the same spreadsheet, so that changes can be seen immediately.
- The concepts of other games such as Catchphrase, Pictionary, and Articulate have all been used to encourage learner engagement.
- Speed dating allows learners to teach each other key aspects of a topic, or share Enterprise ideas, etc.in a fun (and noisy) way.

Reflection point:

1 When planning for lessons how do you spend your most precious resource, i.e. time?
2 How much of your planning time is focused on delivering effective student learning?
3 Are there ways that you can use technology to enable your learners to be more enthused about the subject and take more responsibility for their learning?
4 Are there aspects of your teaching where you can develop re-useable resources?

Trips

Organising trips and visits is always a significant commitment by teachers, and the number of learners who are able to afford to go on a trip beyond the area where they live has fallen in recent years. However, where the department or learners can fund a school trip, then there are a number of organisations that can facilitate these. Some organisations are linked to a particular region; there is a tendency for business trips and visits to be "London-centric." The list below is not an exhaustive list. Nor is it a recommended list. But the list provides a starting point and some ideas of what trips are available:

- Equity School Travel (https://www.equityschooltravel.co.uk/subjects/business-studies)
- NST Group (www.nstgroup.co.uk/business-school-trips)
- Further and Higher Travel (www.fhtgrouptours.com)

Research

Historically, it was unusual for staff to view access to research as being a resource to support teaching. In recent years, this viewpoint is being challenged as can be seen by the rapid growth of ResearchEd (https://researched.org.uk) and the recommendations by the Department for Education both for established teachers and within Initial Teacher Training. Today ResearchEd manages a number of conferences, its own journal, and supports a range of authors who have challenged some of the rhetoric that has been found within teaching. Being able to identify what works, what may work, and what is rhetoric is significant in your continuing development as a teacher.

For example, a significant number of schools applied neurolinguistics planning and the concept of visual, auditory, reading, kinaesthetic (VARK) learners through all subjects - even to the extent that individual learners were being labelled as being a visual learner or a kinaesthetic learner. While there was some benefit in identifying different ways of teaching in order to challenge a monochromic approach, the research community was much more reserved in accepting the approach that was promoted. Given that it was a commercial enterprise behind the promotion of this approach to learning, if a more critical approach had been taken, then many schools would have been able to save significant sums of money, as well as enable learners to have a more rounded understanding of themselves.

Access to research is one of the significant benefits of being attached to a university. In Scotland, this benefit was recognised a few years ago when access to research normally only available to Higher Education staff and students was made available to the teaching profession. For those teachers who are not linked to a university, the following provide some access to research into teaching and learning:

- The Guardian: Reviews of research can be found within the "teacher network; in-depth section" (www.theguardian.com/teacher-network).
- As you would expect TES (www.tes.com) includes articles reviewing research, which are available online, within their weekly publication, and by podcast.
- Various charities that support education are involved in disseminating research. The most famous one is probably the Sutton Trust, which co-supports the Education Endowment Foundation (www.educationfoundation.com), with a key emphasis on social mobility. It has been recommended elsewhere within this book.

- A charity that encourages engagement between business and education, and assesses its impact through research is Education and Employers (www.educationand employers.org). Again, there is an emphasis on supporting learner social mobility.
- Some individuals have developed websites on the basis of their own research into teaching and learning, such as John Hattie and his work on Visible Learning (https://visible-learning.org/john-hattie), Geoff Petty and his work on "Evidence Based Teaching" (www.geoffpetty.com). and Tom Bennett (www.tombennetttraining. co.uk) and his work on Behaviour Management. Someone who is always worth reading is David Didau in his blog on his website called Learning Spy (www.learningspy.co.uk).

It should go without saying that the Department for Education (DfE) also houses significant amounts of information, as well as provides insight into government policy and direction. Ofsted also undertakes surveys and reports, such as the hugely influential 2013 report *Unseen children: educational access and achievement 20 years on*, which investigated education standards in areas with high levels of deprivation.

Conclusion

Being resourceful as a requirement for successful teaching has always been true. The current context for Business and Economics teachers has meant that this is of greater import. The purpose of this chapter has not been to provide an exhaustive list of resources, but as a pointer to reviewing the range of resources that are available to you and to encourage you to consider how to use them to benefit yourself and your learners.

References

Atherton, Peter (2018) *50 Ways to Use Technology Enhanced Learning in the Classroom*. London: Sage Publications.

AQA Education (2019). AQA Realising potential (online). Available from: www.aqa.org.uk [Accessed 24 January 2019]

BBC (2019). BBC News Business (online). Available from: www.bbc.co.uk/news/business [Accessed 24 January 2019]

BBC (2019). *The World of Business Podcasts*. Available from: https://www.bbc.co.uk/programmes/p02nrwfk [Accessed 24 January 2019]

Bee Business Bee Co. UK (2019). BeeBusinessBee (online). Available from: www.youtube.com/user/ beebusinessbee [Accessed 24 January 2019]

Bennett, Tom (2019). Tom Bennett Training Practical & Evidence-Informed Training for Schools (online). Available from: www.tombennetttraining.co.uk [Accessed 24 January 2019]

BusinessEd (2019). BusinessEd Supporting Business Education (online). Available from: www.businessed. co.uk/index.php/home/links [Accessed 24 January 2019]

Business Case Studies (2019). Business Case Studies Teaching Business Studies by Example (online). Available from: http://businesscasestudies.co.uk [Accessed 24 January 2019]

Bloomberg LP (2019). *Bloomberg* (online). Available from: www.bloomberg.com/europe [Accessed 24 January 2019]

Crowther, Barbara (1996). Trading Trainers Game CAFOD (online). Available from: https://www.christianaid.org.uk/sites/default/files/2017-08/trading-trainers-game.pdf [Accessed 24 January 2019]

Gov. UK (2017). Crown Commissioning Service: CCS aggregation (online). Available from: https://www.gov.uk/guidance/ccs-aggregation [Accessed 24 January 2019]

4 Colour Learning Ltd. (2017) Enterprise Village (online). Available from: https://www.achievement-builder.co.uk/ [Accessed 24 January 2019]

Didau, David (2019) The Learning Spy (online). Available from: www.learningspy.co.uk [Accessed 24 January 2019]

EBEA (2017). The Economics, Business and Enterprise Association (EBEA) (online). Available from: https://ebea.org.uk [Accessed 24 January 2019]

Equity School Travel (2019). Business Studies School Trips (online). Available from: https://www.equityschooltravel.co.uk/subjects/business-studies [Accessed 24 January 2019]

Further and Higher Travel (2019). Business Studies and Economics (online). Available from: https://www.fhtgrouptours.com/_s6/business-studies-economics.aspx [Accessed 24 January 2019]

Guardian News and Media Limited (2019). The Guardian Teacher Network (online). Available from: www.theguardian.com/teacher-network [Accessed 24 January 2019]

Hattie, John (2019). Visible Learning. Sebastian Waack, Co-Founder of Edkimo (online). Available from: https://visible-learning.org [Accessed 24 January 2019]

ICAEW (2018). BASE competition (online). Available from: http://careers.icaew.com/campaigns/base-competition [Accessed 23 January 2019]

Issuu Inc. (2019). Issuu (online). Available from: https://issuu.com [Accessed 24 January 2019]

Kahoot! (2019). Kahoot! Make learning awesome! (online). Available from: www.kahoot.com [Accessed 24 January 2019]

LinkedIn Corporation (2019). LinkedIn (online). Available from: www.linkedin.com [Accessed 24 January 2019]

NST Group (2019). The educational travel experts (online). Available from: www.nstgroup.co.uk [Accessed 24 January 2019]

Ofsted (2013). Unseen children: access and achievement 20 years on. Crown Copyright (online). Available from: https://www.gov.uk/government/publications/unseen-children-access-and-achievement-20-years-on [Accessed 24 January 2019]

OCR (2019). OCR Oxford Cambridge and RSA (online). Available from: www.ocr.org.uk [Accessed 24 January 2019]

Pearson (2019). Business, Administration and Law (online). Available from: https://qualifications.pearson.com/en/subjects/business.html [Accessed 24 January 2019]

Prezi Inc. (2019). Prezi (online). Available from: https://prezi.com [Accessed 24 January 2019]

Petty, Geoff (2019). Geoff Petty: Improve your teaching and that of your team (online). Available from: www.geoffpetty.com [Accessed 24 January 2019]

Research Ed. (2019). (online). Available from: https://researched.org.uk [Accessed 28 January 2019]

S-cool Youth Marketing Ltd. (2018). S-cool the revision website: Business studies revision (online). Available from: www.s-cool.co.uk/a-level/business-studies [Accessed 24 January 2019]

Scoop it! (2019). Research and publish the best content (online). Available from: www.scoop.it [Accessed 24 January 2019]

Socrative (2019). Socrative (online). Available from: www.socrative.com [Accessed 24 January 2019]

TES (2019). *TES I want to teach.* (online). Available from: www.tes.com [Accessed 24 January 2019]

The Chartered College of Teaching (2019). Chartered College of Teaching (online). Available from: https://chartered.college [Accessed 24 January 2019]

The Economist Newspaper Ltd (2019). *The Economist* (online). Available from: www.economist.com [Accessed 24 January 2019]

The Financial Times Group (2019). *The Financial Times* (online). Available from: www.ft.com [Accessed 24 January 2019]

The London Institute of Banking and Finance (2018). Student Investor Challenge (online). Available from: http://www.studentinvestor.org [Accessed 23 January 2019]

The Sutton Trust (2011). The Education Endowment Foundation (online). Available from: https://educationendowmentfoundation.org.uk/ [Accessed 24 January 2019]

Tutor2u (2019). The Exam Performance Specialists (online). Available from: https://www.tutor2u.net [Accessed 24 January 2019]

UCLES (2018). Cambridge Assessment International Education (online). Available from: www.cambridgeinternational.org [Accessed 24 January 2019]

Young Enterprise (2019). Young Money (online). Available from: www.young-money.org.uk [Accessed 23 January 2019]

WJEC CBAC (2019) (online). Available from www.wjec.co.uk [Accessed 24 January 2019]

WJEC (2019) Eduqas (online). Available from: https://www.eduqas.co.uk [Accessed 24 January 2019]

9

THE REFLECTIVE PRACTITIONER

The place of reflection in the continuous development of programmes and practitioners

- An introduction to professional reflection and why it is important
- The place of ethics
- Evidence-based practice: making evaluation count

    - i. Working with a mentor
    - ii. Review of learning
    - iii. Peer review
    - iv. Reflection on practice
    - v. Using research evidence to inform your teaching
    - vi. Research of practice

- Networking and developing a community of practice
- The Master's profession
- Conclusion

An introduction to professional reflection and why it is important

A colleague was appointed as Head of Department (HoD) at a school that had been looking for a new HoD for over a year. Whilst the school had undertaken a number of interviews during this time, no one had been offered the position before. So why was she successful? The school has a very multicultural intake and as part of the interview she was asked to teach a lesson to a Year 10 class, which turned out to be all boys. The reasons she gave for being offered the post related to the opportunities she had pursued previously which had enabled her to do a systematic investigation of her teaching and pupil learning. During her teacher training year, the PGCE, she had been required to undertake a research project. She had chosen to do a research project on the theme of "How to engage boys." After she had finished the PGCE, and was teaching she completed a Master's degree on the theme of minority ethnic teaching within a sixth form context. The two pieces of research had enabled her to develop high order skills that fitted her for the role as a new HoD in that school.

While it was Socrates who said *"An unexamined life is not worth living,"* it was the Enlightenment that brought us the belief that mankind is able to improve itself. Events in the news may cause us to challenge this worldview. However, I would argue that as teachers it is the case that we are able to learn from our mistakes, learn from our successes and learn from others who are more expert than we are ourselves, and thereby improve our practice. Knowing we are able to constantly improve our practice is one of those aspects of teaching that means our love of learning is never diminished – and this idea maintains our enthusiasm for the profession. Moreover, identifying those approaches that have genuine impact on learning will mean that planning and assessment will be more focused and more efficient, and therefore supports the development of a work-life balance.

As well as the intrinsic motivation as professionals to continually improve our practice, the impetus to become Reflective Practitioners and to participate in Continuing Professional Development (CPD) is also extrinsic and comes from a variety of quarters. Ofsted now expects schools to show that their approaches to teaching and learning are evidence-based. The Department for Education (DfE) supports the development of the Education Endowment Foundation (EEF), and there are calls for schools to be involved in research projects. This is in addition to the research that both the DfE and Ofsted undertake for their own purposes. In the recent past, there were calls for teaching to become a Master's profession. Those universities that deliver teacher training often have further CPD available, which can include accreditation routes that build up to a Masters or doctoral study. In the university that I work in this goes further with opportunities for professional accreditation, including that required to be a Special Educational Needs Coordinator (SENCO) and specialist study for dyslexia and dyscalculia. At the time of writing, the Early Career Framework is in development and there is an investigation into what opportunities for career development exist and should exist for every teacher, not just those who are wanting to pursue a career in management. Much of this has arisen as a result of the widespread awareness that buying commercial approaches to teaching and learning – e.g. Kagan – does not necessarily result in automatic increases in learner achievement.

Even in the mainstream press, there is an increased expectation for teaching and learning to be based on evidence. In some cases, schools are responding to this expectation by the development of a Research Lead within the teaching staff. The role of the Research Lead is to sift through research as it becomes publicly available and identify what is appropriate for discussion as part of CPD within the school. In some instances, the Research Lead is also responsible for the development of individual action research projects. The purpose of an individual action research project is to introduce a change to the way a subject is delivered and to evaluate the impact of that new initiative and its transferability across the school. Moreover, the newly formed Chartered College of Teaching seeks to provide accreditation for the development of excellence in teaching through the use of evidence-based approaches.

There is another reason for being actively involved in the development of your own practice that is to maintain or develop a sense of autonomy and agency in your own classroom. Senior management within schools always carry responsibility for the results of the learners in the school, and it is not unusual that the way they deal with this is by exerting control in the classroom practices of their staff. Investigating your practice is one way of taking back control of your own teaching, and of protecting your own mental well-being. Working with colleagues, this need for professional autonomy is particularly strong amongst teachers that feel the need to defend themselves and their subject to senior management as they are not considered to be core to the curriculum, largely because of external pressures such as Progress 8. Developing this personal autonomy supports not only your teaching, but also your ability to represent your subject by having a clear rationale for its inclusion into the curriculum.

There are different ways in which you can investigate and develop your own practice. This chapter seeks to provide a simple introduction to some approaches that will support your continuing development within this profession. There are other texts that provide much more detailed introductions to the place of research within the classroom and need to be investigated before undertaking any significant research project.

We will begin with the place of systematic evaluation and the different ways that this can be undertaken. We will then move onto the value of collaboration - or networking - which can be within your school or with those working in the same area but in other schools. Then the third approach we will look at is through more formal accreditation of systematic evaluation by gaining a Master's qualification. There will be those who will go on to undertake doctoral study, either a PhD (Doctor of Philosophy) or EdD (Doctor of Education). However, investigating doctoral study is beyond the remit of this chapter. There are different routes to obtaining your doctorate. If this is something that appeals, then I would recommend speaking to someone in your local Higher Education teacher-training provider.

The place of ethics

However informal or formal development or investigation of teaching is undertaken ethical considerations need to be accounted for. This is particularly the case in schools as it involves learners who are considered to be vulnerable participants. This is because, as young people, they are not in a position to provide fully informed consent and where their relationship with you is not equal, i.e. as the teacher you are always in a position of power relative to the learner. In addition, the data may be sensitive and may have implications for those you teach and work with. Participants, i.e. your learners and colleagues, need to be protected, and they need to feel secure that they will not be disadvantaged as a result of the investigation process or findings. The more formal the investigation or development, the more rigorous the approach to ethics is required.

Evidence-based practice: making evaluation count

As indicated earlier, our review of Reflective Practice will begin with the place of systematic evaluation of our own practice. This is often described as becoming a Reflective Practitioner, where reflection is the mode of development.

There are a variety of views about what reflection is, and the following typology (Ghaye, Tony, 2011) will help to unpick this:

- The first approach is called **Reflection-IN-action**. Most teachers will undertake this reflection without being aware of this. It is where you adapt your lesson in response to learner feedback and undertaken during the lesson. Some may call this "thinking on your feet" or improvisation. When learning to teach, there is a definite point when the new teacher realises that "sticking to the plan" does not always work, if ever, and that the delivery of the lesson will have to change to enable learners to engage and make progress.
- The second approach is called **Reflection-ON-practice**. This reflection is undertaken *after* the event, usually after the lesson and when something significant has occurred - either good or bad. It causes the teacher to stop and consider why that event occurred

and how to respond. This may mean that the perspective of the teacher changes in terms of his/her own practice or of the teacher's understanding of learners or the class.

- The third approach is called **Reflection–FOR–practice**. Here there is a particular reason for undertaking this reflection and it will result in a planned response. It may follow directly from the previous category of **Reflection–ON–practice**, as future planning is based upon initial reflections.
- The final approach is called **Reflection–WITH–action.** Here there is a conscious sense of planning for future significant actions, such as changing a qualification in order to suit learners better and give them improved opportunities for success. This approach may have an impact that is wider than just for yourself. The example given would have repercussions for the wider course team and for learners as well.

As you read these, you may find yourself identifying or recognising the different approaches from your own experiences. Furthermore, you may find these overlap or bleed into each other. The following provides practical approaches to reflect, to review, and to evaluate your development. Each approach has a value in its own right, but requires different levels of engagement in its own practice and in the expertise that is available outside of your own classroom.

i. Working with a mentor

During the first two years of teaching – including your teacher-training course, whether that is a PGCE or an apprenticeship or working towards a Further Education (FE) teaching qualification, or even if you are teaching as an unqualified teacher – you should be allocated a subject-specific mentor within the department where you are working. The role of this person is to be able to guide you through those first experiences of teaching the subject within their school or college.

The style of mentoring varies and can be dependent upon the sector you are training within and the sector you are training for: 11 to 16 high school, 11 to 18 high school, sixth form college, or FE College. Within the school sector, we have seen the introduction of Mentoring Standards for school-based initial teacher training (2016), which has been a welcome addition to the process of supporting and training mentors. Whatever the context, there are expectations about how the mentoring relationship will change and develop to support a new teacher to become an effective and reflective practitioner.

At the start of the process, your relationship with the mentor will be close and you should expect regular meetings and formal observations of your teaching. There will also be informal observations, including those by other members of staff. The meetings with your mentor will allow you to pull together feedback from observations of your teaching, both formal and informal, and reflect on your progress.

In these early meetings, the mentor will set the pace and tone of those meetings, taking on the role of an expert and model practitioner. This will be reflected in the way the mentor manages these meetings, often being direct in the targets that are being set on a weekly basis. As the year develops, the relationship with the mentor should change as he/she supports you to become an independent and reflective practitioner in your own right. Therefore, there is an expectation that by the end of the first year, the pace and tone of the mentor meetings should be led by you, as you are able to identify the strengths and areas of development in your own practice. At this stage, an expert mentor will be asking questions to tease out your own thinking and decision making, rather than telling you what to do. Therefore, when you enter your second year of teaching, you will know what questions you should be asking of yourself to continue the progress made in Year 1.

The nature of teacher training in England is that it is largely performative, and so there is a framework that both you and the mentor are working with to support your development, i.e. The Teachers' Standards (2013), for those training to teach within the secondary school sector and the Professional Standards for the FE Teacher (2014). Progress against these standards will be formally assessed at key points during the first year using evidence provided by the trainee teacher and in discussion with the trainee teacher, the school-based or college-based mentors, and the Higher Education Institution (HEI)/ university provider. In the school sector, Qualified Teacher Status (QTS) is awarded at the end of that first year of initial teacher training – to be confirmed at the end of their probationary period when they are known as a Newly Qualified Teacher (NQT).

In the second year of teaching, you will still have a mentor who will continue to monitor your development, which will include undertaking formal observations as well as continuing to track your progress against the Teachers' Standards (2013) or the Professional Standards for the FE Teacher (2014). In the school sector, at this stage you will be known as a Newly Qualified Teacher (NQT), and then as a Recently Qualified Teacher (RQT). For the teacher within the FE sector, training does not formally conclude until the end of the second year. For both sectors, mentoring is far more at arm's length when compared to the first year of teaching. You will continue to be supported by the teachers that you are working alongside, including your HoD, and you will find those people who are able to answer questions that you have and provide advice and guidance.

Although the current requirement for a school or college to provide you with a mentor will stop at the end of the second year, formal observations of your teaching will continue. These will be undertaken by HoDs and senior leaders, and they will usually be linked to performance review.

It is anticipated that in the schools' sector the introduction of the Early Career Framework will result in a more structured process of support for new teachers with more robust expectations for the provision of CPD. Alongside this is the expectation that QTS will be awarded at the end of the probationary period of teaching, rather than the confirmation of the award which is the present position.

While the school or college is unlikely to formally provide you with a mentor after those first two years, teaching has followed the move to the use of mentors as an established element of career development, as in other professions. A significant number of teachers, at all stages of their careers, continue to seek out mentors to support and guide them. This is not a sign of weakness, but it is more often a sign of strength and a commitment to the profession. It provides a more formalised forum for discussion which is focused on the significant questions that you have at the time and uses the expertise that is available beyond the school. For many, it provides clear direction on how to manage new roles or to seek career opportunities.

ii. Review of learning

Most teachers will say that they engage in evaluation of their own teaching. This will start with individual lessons and working out what seems to work and what doesn't; this is often in terms of behaviour or engagement, despite the current emphasis of "progress" within schools. A simple way of capturing this is by annotating schemes of work or lesson plans as recommended in Chapter 2 "Getting started: teaching academic subjects" and Chapter 3 "Getting started: teaching vocational subjects." Student teachers are usually expected to review each lesson, sometimes by being directed to ask questions similar to those below:

- **What have learners learnt?** How do I know? What do they need to review in the next lesson to embed learning? What stretch and challenge do I need to incorporate?
- **What behaviours have been exhibited?** How have I positively influenced behaviour? Am I encouraging learners to be curious? Do I need to set out my boundaries more clearly? Have I used the school behaviour policy effectively?
- **Is my subject knowledge secure enough?** Is it good enough to provide stretch and challenge? Where are learners expected to develop skills of analysis and evaluation? How does it link to the specification?

By looking through these lesson reviews and annotations of lesson plans and schemes of work at regular intervals it can mean that approaches can be considered and adapted.

Sometimes there will be a more formal review at the end of each module or term, based on learner feedback and learner achievement. These may be linked to school data tracking systems. The evaluations can be used for school reporting purposes. At the end of each year, the HoD will review the performance of the department, which is usually based on learner achievement and staff performance reviews. This approach to evaluation is good, but it could be better by being more systematic. The following section introduces different approaches to being more focussed in developing professional practice.

iii. Peer review

There are a variety of approaches to peer review – with an equal variety of impact.

At the very start of your teaching career you will spend time observing a wide range of teachers with a variety of classes and you will be able to sense which teachers are good, and which are excellent. You may even feel that you know why they are good or excellent. Unfortunately, the opportunity to observe teaching diminishes over time as the responsibilities of a new teacher increase. Despite this, there is a lot to commend the regular updating of practice through observation. Many good schools encourage staff to observe each other – informally – in order to see how their learners behave in different classes, as well as to find and develop new techniques for their own classrooms. (It is always very flattering to be asked to be observed by a colleague - so don't be afraid to ask, whatever stage of your career!) While this may be considered to be a form of peer review, it is very informal, and the level of impact on your practice and on others can be limited.

A more structured and more meaningful form of peer review is when colleagues work together on a particular aspect of practice. Sometimes management are closely involved with the development of peer review - choosing who a teacher works with and what the focus of peer review is. Sometimes management are more "hands off" allowing staff to identify who they want to work with and what to investigate, which could be because of subject expertise or pedagogical knowledge or interest. For example, as financial capability is a small part of the GCSE Maths curriculum, it would be useful to work with a maths teacher on some key financial concepts – using the expertise of both subject specialists to develop an aspect of the curriculum that is nominally common to both Business and Maths qualifications. It could lead to your development of how to teach individual maths concepts and enable the maths teacher to develop questions that relate to real-life financial concepts. Pedagogical models are likely to be quite different, with Business and Economics more likely to use case studies and inquiry-led learning, whereas the teaching of Maths can often be more didactic.

An alternative may be to investigate different forms of assessment of learners. I had colleagues from different qualifications who investigated *the use of presentations*. This resulted in assumptions and perspectives being challenged for both teachers. As a result, they developed a wider understanding of what it meant for students to undertake presentations (What is a presentation?), new approaches to supporting learners in their ability to plan and deliver presentations, and different ways of assessing the quality of presentations.

As a new teacher you may want to investigate ways in which you can manage your workload within your peer review. This is being very pragmatic, but potentially significant for your well-being and longevity within the profession.

When you have ownership and control of peer review, it can be a very powerful tool for your own development. It doesn't always work the first time around. It can take time to develop the expertise to make this work well in order to identify which colleagues are the ones that you want to work with so that you will be able to maximise the benefits of the process, and to find colleagues who are prepared to be both collaborative and collegial, i.e. to work with you and to be supportive.

iv. Reflection on practice

On PGCE courses, there is usually at least one module that expects the student teacher to reflect on a particular aspect of his/her practice, e.g. behaviour with the Year 10 GCSE Business class, or higher order questioning with the Year 12 A level class. To be successful, student teachers will be expected to read around the subject, to apply it to their practice within their particular placement context, and to review the impact on learner learning. To do this successfully requires a readiness to do the necessary reading so student teachers can become *expert* in that topic and are able to critically assess different approaches to identify which approach is most beneficial within their context. It requires a real humility in their learning – to know that they may be wrong and, therefore, need to amend their concept of learners as well as change their practice. It may also require courage if deepening their understanding results in challenging the accepted norms of practice within the department or school.

The formal name for this process is **Experiential Learning** and it goes beyond the evaluation of sessions because it requires a more structured approach. There are a number of different models that can be adopted to support this structured approach. The approach that I am using is my adaptation of David Kolb's Experiential Learning Cycle - Concrete experience, Reflective observation, Abstract conceptualisation, and Active experimentation –which allows for successive cycles for learning. This is often presented visually, as shown in Figure 9.1.

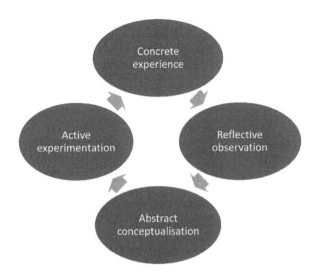

Figure 9.1 Kolb's model of Experiential Learning.

Concrete experience is usually that point where the teacher recognises that what he/ she is doing in the classroom is not working or is not working as well as he/she would like it to. This results in a sense of uncertainty – or occasionally crisis – which leads the teacher to participate in **Reflective observation** and further investigation into the situation. To reflectively observe means to step back from the immediate emotions of the situation and to begin to consider that there may be other ways of viewing the situation:

- What is it about learners that is acting as a barrier to their learning?
- Is it about the environment?
- Is it about your own preconceptions or attitudes?
- Is it about the way you are delivering the lesson?

This can be hard as it means questioning yourself as well as learners and then accepting that change needs to happen.

In my application of Kolb's Experiential Learning Cycle, **Abstract conceptualisation** is that point where there the teacher takes the initiative to investigate what is going on beyond the classroom and may relate to student learning (pedagogy) or the curriculum being delivered. This often begins by talking with other staff in school. In terms of student learning, this is usually the SENCo, the Special Needs and Disability Coordinator, as well as other key figures to see what influencing factors are at work, whether there are trends, and what successful strategies are being used elsewhere that could be adopted. In terms of curriculum, this may be other people in the department or those who deliver a similar qualification within the school. In addition, there is a significant range of materials that are freely available online, as well as texts that can be bought that allow for the wider investigation of the issue. These allow the teacher to understand alternative perspectives more deeply and what may be appropriate for that context.

An example of when a teacher may want to investigate an issue more widely would be with a disadvantaged child who is failing to make good progress within the class.

Schools are now held to account for the money that they receive for disadvantaged learners and many schools use this money on Maths and English intervention or school-wide initiatives. For the class teacher (not in English and Maths), further investigation may be needed to identify strategies that are specific to their own lessons:

- Are there other issues apart from the child being disadvantaged?
- Are there behaviour management approaches that may be used, but not included in the school policy?
- Are there other ways of differentiating materials that you have not considered?
- Are there ways of making learners feel safe in your class so that they can ask questions and take on board what is being taught?

There are a range of sources of good material that can be accessed that will enable the teacher to consider the issue from different perspectives, including:

- Daisy Christodoulou's *Making Good Progress: The future of Assessment for Learning*, the Education Endowment Foundation (www.educationendowmentfoundation.org.uk).
- David Didau's The Learning Spy (www.learningspy.co.uk).
- John Hattie's *Visible Learning* (https://visible-learning.org/john-hattie/).
- researchED (https://researched.org.uk/).

By investigating the issue from alternative perspectives, the teacher will be able to identify approaches that they are prepared to experiment with in their own classroom. Within Kolb's Experiential Learning Cycle this stage is called **Active experimentation,** where a teacher introduces the new approach. Following this, the teacher will be able to reflect on whether or not the approach works. If the approach doesn't work – or it doesn't work as well as hoped – then another cycle of Experiential Learning can be engaged with.

Developing a critical eye when reading more widely, whether this is research or more populist materials, is necessary. There are many examples within education where the latest "research" has been latched onto and applied without investigating the source and quality of the underlying material. One example is the idea that learners remember 5 percent of what they are told but 90 percent of what they teach others. Another example is that learners have particular learning styles called VARK Modalities, labelled as Visual, Auditory, Read/write, and Kinaesthetic. Both examples have encouraged an increased variety in teaching methods. However, in each case the underlying evidence is minimal and there are many research studies that significantly undermine the claims of learning styles. Despite this their use is still prevalent.

As I write this book, **Direct Instruction** is an approach that is receiving recognition for its successes. With any "research," the message is that you need to tread carefully and find out what the background to that research is:

- Was it used with particular students in certain circumstances?
- What was the sample size?
- Is it a commercial enterprise?
- Do you really understand what the research is saying?
- Is it appropriate for my context?

Working only with the headlines of what is popular at the moment will lead to disappointment and cynicism regarding research and evidence-based practice generally.

Reflective practice may be something that as a practitioner you already identify with or you may be looking for alternative ways of reflecting on practice. In the first instance, I would suggest other texts that look at different ways of developing reflective practice be considered, such as:

- Sue Dymoke's *Reflective Teaching and Learning in the Secondary School (Developing as a Reflective Secondary Teacher,* 2nd ed.
- Andrew Pollard's *Reflective Teaching in Schools*, 5th ed.

By doing this, you are engaging at a deeper level by assessing the impact of practice, or change in practice to a more rigorous degree, which can become a stepping stone to researching practice in a more rigorous way.

v. Using research evidence to inform your teaching

The approach taken above is one where a teacher has a particular issue that he/she wants to investigate and *takes the issue to the research*, i.e. to identify examples of research that have been undertaken in relation to the issue being considered. An alternative approach is to *take the research to the teaching*. This would mean that by reading, discussing, and analysing research, then the teaching is adapted in the light of what has been learnt. This is widely considered to be an advantage of undertaking a University based teacher training programme where student teachers have both access to extensive research and time (in relative terms) to evaluate the quality of research, and to consider its relevance to the context within which they teach.

This approach has gained significantly in popularity, both from the viewpoint of the establishment and by the rapid growth of researchEd (www.ResearchEd.org.uk), which attracts significant numbers of teachers to its relaxed and informal conferences that blend current research from a variety of fields - including Psychology and Neuroscience - with teachers' experiences in the classroom. Interest in research is also fueled by the increasing accessibility to research. This is partly due to the internet (as indicated in the number of websites referred to in this text). In addition to the internet is the access to research that comes from twitter and, to a lesser extent, LinkedIn.

The backing for the use of evidence-based or research-based practices can be seen in the significant investment in the Education Endowment Foundation (EEF) (www.educationendowmentfoundation.org.uk) by the Department for Education. A visit to the website provides you with access to a range of approaches that have been assessed for their impact with access to the underpinning research, some of which is better than others. More recently, The Education Endowment Foundation has been instrumental in the development of Research Schools, which are involved in research projects looking at key governmental priorities, such as social mobility and the attainment gap between disadvantaged children and those who are not disadvantaged. It is now being seen in the development of the Early Career Framework which will require teachers to continue to engage in.

In earlier chapters, you were introduced to a wide range of learning theories, each of which have a part to play in understanding the breadth and complexity of the teaching role – but also adds to the dynamic nature of who we are and what we are about. There is a tension held between being overwhelmed with the amount of information that is available and pretending that it doesn't exist by believing that your own experience is the only thing that matters – or that those populist books are enough.

vi. Research of practice

An even more rigorous approach to investigating the impact of your teaching is through the use of a formal research project. There are different ways in which practice can be researched, and with different reasons for doing so. It can simply be a way of improving the delivery of the subject in the classroom, by taking into account learners who are being taught. However, it can be a way of enhancing a teacher's profile within the school, or for a broader network. In some instances, undertaking research is a way to enhance the profile of a school, such as becoming involved in the development of research schools.

This section is *not* going to provide you with detailed guidance on how to undertake a formal research project, but it will highlight the impact that can be achieved by doing this. For example, if you want to assess the impact of an intervention, then an approach that could be considered is that of using **action research methodology**. To do this well requires that you:

- See what has been written about the approach that you are considering.
- Identify what is good about that approach.
- Decide whether or not that approach will be appropriate for your context.
- Determine what are the issues.
- Etc.

You will need to identify what impact you want to measure, how you will measure it, and how long you will run the intervention for – before and after the application of the intervention. After the intervention, you can measure the impact to see if the intervention was effective and then use the literature to analyse your findings. Rigorous evaluations will be useful for this level of research, including learner voice, learner data, etc. Remember that ethics is important, so the identity of all participants is should be kept hidden from wider view. This approach allows you to dive more deeply into the extent of the impact of the intervention, why the intervention works – or does not work – and to decide whether it can be transferred to other groups or contexts.

Investigating the impact of a change in teaching or an intervention can be done using an approach called **Action Research.** An example of where I used this approach is when I was asked to put on additional sessions for A level Business students that I didn't teach. I was asked to deliver one session a week, each lasting for one hour, over half a term. A key aspect that came out of the literature review was that there had to be consistency in the approach with the remainder of their lessons for the intervention to be successful. As I taught the students, it became clear that the approach that I was taking in terms of the way that I was assessing their work and the feedback I was providing – both of which were closely linked to the qualification assessment criteria - was very different from that of their normal teacher, and that they were struggling to implement what I was saying. This was very evident in the data that came from the questions set in class and from the conversations that I was having with learners. Consequently, the impact was very limited, although the HoD was clearly pleased that the learners at least passed the exam! However, it is still the case that some additional research into the literature could have led to better planning for the intervention and resulted in better grades for the learners. It also explains why much intervention is successful when undertaken by the class teacher.

The example I have provided is a very simple version of Action Research and one that can be implemented relatively easily. To investigate Action Research further, I recommend Mary McAteer's book *Action Research in Education*.

There are different approaches to research in education. To provide a contrast, a piece of research that had a much more successful outcome was around the theme of **outstanding coursework lessons,** led by my colleague Jill McKenzie (2016). In this instance, a different research methodology was used. We had worked with a number of schools that delivered a variety of coursework-based qualifications. When undertaking observations of trainee teachers, it was not unusual to receive the request for the observations of coursework lessons to be avoided. On occasion, some mentors had even indicated that it was impossible to deliver an outstanding coursework lesson. Consequently, an exploratory qualitative study was undertaken, i.e. practice was explored both by investigating the literature – populist as well as academic – as well as undertaking semi-structured interviews with Heads of Departments (HoDs), class teachers, and a focus group with student teachers. A qualitative approach was used as opinions were being investigated in order to gain a deeper understanding of what approaches could be used to provide the best learning experience within the classroom.

As a result of synthesising her findings, Jill McKenzie was able to develop an understanding and guidance on how to plan and deliver coursework lessons that enabled all learners to make excellent progress – and for it to be enjoyable. This has then fed into our discussions with teachers, delivery on the PGCE that we co-delivered, as well as a jointly authored article within the EBEA journal *Teaching Business & Economics.*

In both cases, a similar structure to the research was undertaken:

a   Identifying the focus of the investigation and ethical considerations for the people who are being researched.

b   Undertaking a literature review, i.e. reading as much as possible about the subject to find out what was already known and where the gaps are. Deciding if this changed the focus of the research.

c   Deciding how to investigate the "problem." Action research? Case study? Systematic review? Mixed methods? What methods to use: Quantitative and/ or qualitative? Data (before and after intervention)? Interviews? Focus groups? Questionnaires? etc.

d   What ethical considerations need to be taken into account? How do these affect the management of the project?

e   Collecting and collating the data (which includes the transcripts of interviews as well as quantitative material)

f   Analysing the data. Using the expertise that has been garnered from the literature review, as well as your own critical thinking.

g   Conclusions and their impact on your teaching/professional development.

This is not enough information for you to be able to undertake a research project. To be able to ensure that when undertaking research you use your time effectively and efficiently, I recommend that you read the following books about how to undertake research projects:

- Nicholas Walliman's *Your Research Project: A Step-by-Step Guide for the First Time Researcher,* 3rd ed.
- Jon Swain's *Designing Research in Education: Concepts and Methodologies.*

As indicated earlier, ethics is an important consideration, particularly so with a formal research structure. Participants need to feel secure in order to enable you to obtain the best information that you can – whether or not it provides the results that you or the school want to hear. To pursue this further, I recommend that the British Education Research Association (BERA) guidelines be used. They can be accessed at: https://www.bera.ac.uk/publication/ethical-guidelines-for-educational-research-2018.

Both pieces of research obviously had impact – even if the results weren't what we wanted to hear! It enabled us to work closely with the network of teachers from different schools and experience the benefits of networking. Who to network with is addressed in the next part of this chapter.

Reflection point:

1 How do you feel when you hear the term *research*?
2 In what ways do you think that your own practice has been influenced by research?
3 Is there something that you would like to experiment with or investigate to improve your student learning?
4 How autonomous do you feel in how you teach?

Networking and developing a community of practice

One of the reasons for taking control of your own practice through Continuing Professional Development (CPD), Active reflection, and research is to develop a sense of professional autonomy and agency – particularly within what can be a very stressful environment. The approaches identified already require engaging with others within your profession, either within your school or with colleagues in other schools and institutions. Another way of managing your own development and ensuring that your practices are up-to-date AND provides you with support and encouragement is through developing a Community of Practice (CoP) or network. In the past, this was something that Ofsted has indicated that Business and Economics teachers don't do enough of and yet the benefits are significant. The existence of online/social media has enabled networks to develop more easily and it is useful to make the most of these.

There are a variety of networks that exist or can be developed. A fuller discussion of this is in Chapter 8 "Maximising the use of resources." In many cases, these networks exist around the delivery of a particular qualification. This can be through links to the exam board and the various CPD opportunities that they provide. Some staff get involved with the exam boards through exam marking, which is a great way of really finding out what the exam board is looking for from your learners. Another way is through other organisations such as the Facebook BTEC group, which is managed by tutor2u. In some areas, schools work together and will facilitate meetings between Heads of Department (HoDs) to develop and share good practice.

The professional association for Business and Economics teachers is the Economics, Business and Enterprise Association (EBEA). The association offers both individual and corporate memberships and the EBEA is recommended by the HMI for Ofsted for the subject area. As well as the provision of a quarterly journal with articles covering both subject knowledge and pedagogy, and reviews of resources, there are regular opportunities to participate in webinars, where you can discuss what Ofsted is looking for, questions about Enterprise, etc. Becoming involved with the EBEA can lead to other opportunities, such as writing for the journal or leading webinars yourself, and being involved in other aspects of the association. All of these can be useful in developing your professional profile, which can assist in your career development. While all of these are incredibly useful for the day-to-day business of teaching your subject(s), a further significant aspect of the EBEA is that it is the mouthpiece for the profession and is regularly called upon to participate in consultations from government and the Department for Education (DfE) on behalf of business and economics teachers.

Increasingly, teachers are taking responsibility for their own CPD, both within schools and beyond their school environment. Part of this is fuelled by the accessibility of networks and research that comes through the use of social media and the Internet. This is seen in the development of subject-specific Facebook groups, and hashtags on Twitter. It is also seen in the development of the unconference, i.e. gatherings of teachers that are noted for their enthusiasm and informality. Examples include the teachmeet and researchEd conferences - both of which can be searched for with the #teachmeet or #researchEd on Twitter. There are differences in focus between the two approaches to CPD. The teachmeet tends to be focused on developing teaching techniques and has a significant input in terms of technology-enhanced learning. researchEd has a clear focus on the use of research to inform teaching. It is not just a case of pedagogical research, i.e. what works in the classroom, but it draws from research in Psychology and Neuroscience. to give insight into learners and thereby enable teachers to adapt their expectations and practice in the light of that.

Another way of networking is by working with your local University - particularly if they deliver teacher training and/or have a Business school as part of their provision. Working with a University that delivers teacher training is particularly useful with the increase in expectations on school and college-based staff to be involved with research. There are departments that work with their trainee teachers on placement to undertake mini-research projects and making the most of their access to support from University staff and library resources. In some cases this relationship with the University is specifically linked to school improvement planning and will mean that trained researchers work with school staff. An example of this has been where school based staff are trained in lesson study. This approach is a way of structuring the development of collaborative evaluation following collaborative planning of teaching. Working with one school in special measures this resulted in a significant empowering of staff in what was a challenging context with positive impact on their learners.

The Master's profession

In recent years – yet at different times in different parts of the United Kingdom and Ireland – there has been an enthusiasm to make teaching a Master's profession. The aim has been to raise the status of the profession as well as to improve the skills of the teaching staff and learner learning. For the individual teacher, undertaking a Master's in Education provides them with opportunities to raise their profile within the department or school and it is useful for pursuing promotion, as indicated at the start of this chapter. It is also a way of refining and developing practice within the classroom for yourself and for your colleagues. It provides you with access to a huge range of free resources in terms of access to texts, many of which are electronic and are not available without being a member of a University (unless you are in Scotland). In addition, it allows you to develop your skills in research, so that investigating teaching can be both rigorous AND efficient in terms of the time that it takes to undertake this and formulate your conclusions.

A number of Universities offer the opportunity to undertake a Master's in Education, particularly if they already offer teacher training. It may be that you wish to return to the University where you completed your teacher training, if appropriate. It may be that you want to develop expertise in a particular area, such as dyslexia. It is always worth having a look at other Universities to investigate their provision, both in terms of content and delivery, to ensure that what you want to get out of the qualification matches what is being offered. In terms of content it is very important that you study a research methods module. This introduces you to a much deeper understanding of how to approach research – including ethical considerations – and usually allows you to use this as a way of setting up the final research project. It means that the last module is much more efficient in terms of your time and the results are more professionally satisfying.

Approaches to the way that a Master's qualification is delivered vary widely and it can be difficult to know what questions to ask when deciding where to study. As a teacher, you will want part-time provision and an online course may seem to be very attractive. Blended delivery (part face-to-face and part online) is common and is an approach that allows for the development of peer support, greater interaction with tutors and an increased level of motivation. It is normal for there to be an online aspect to the delivery of any University study, but it should not mean that the resources are kept in an electronic repository which you only access when you want, usually as a deadline is approaching. There should be opportunities to discuss subject material, to obtain formative feedback, and to learn to self-assess your work. Such approaches make the process easier and more enjoyable – and less lonely! Whatever delivery model you choose, please investigate the support that you receive and how this operates. If online, what tutorial support exists and how often do you meet (electronically or face-to-face)? If you have not undertaken a PGCE before, what support exists to support your return to academic writing and at a post-graduate level?

If you have undertaken a PGCE, then it is probable you have already undertaken modules that attract Level 7/Master's level credits. Where this is the case, it is worth investigating the University that you are intending to study for your Master's at to see if these credits can be transferred in order to reduce the number of modules that you need to undertake in order to complete the qualification. This is called Accreditation of Prior Learning (APL).

For the few who wish to pursue a doctorate in Education (or other higher degree), then you will need to decide what sort of doctorate you want to pursue, PhD or EdD. While a Master's qualification is not a requirement to pursuing a doctorate, many choose to do a Master's in Research (MRes) as a preparation for the PhD. Others may choose to undertake a taught PhD, which means that the first part of the PhD is made up of a number of modules that prepare the student for their final piece of research. For others, who have a clearer idea of what they want to research then the more traditional PhD may be the appropriate route for them. As well as different models of doctoral study, the level and quality of supervision (support) can vary. As can be seen the range of approaches is significant and expert advice will need to be sought.

Reflection point:

1 How do you view yourself as a teacher?
2 What does it mean to you to be a professional?
3 How do you want to develop your career?
4 What do you want to improve – your teaching, student learning, or perhaps the staff within your department?

Conclusion

This chapter has touched on a number of different approaches to improving and developing professional practice. To pursue the development of your skills will require further reading and investigation, suggestions for which are given in the text. Underpinning your approach will be how you view yourself as a teacher and how you wish your career to develop. It may be that you want to become a senior leader within a school, or maybe that you want to stay in the classroom in order to have maximum direct impact on your learners. Either way, improving practice is key for you and for those who work with you.

References

British Education Research Association (2018) Ethical Guidelines for Educational Research (online). Available from https://www.bera.ac.uk/publication/ethical-guidelines-for-educational-research-2018 [Accessed 22nd August 2019]

Carter, Andrew (2015). Carter review of initial teacher training (ITT). Crown Copyright DFE-00036-2015 (online). Available from: https://assets.publishing.service.gov.uk/government/uploads/system/uploads/attachment_data/file/399957/Carter_Review.pdf [Accessed 28 January 2019]

Christodoulou, Daisy (2017). *Making Good Progress: The future of Assessment for Learning*. Oxford: Oxford University Press.

Department for Education (2013). The Teachers' Standards (online). Available from: https://assets.publishing.service.gov.uk/government/uploads/system/uploads/attachment_data/file/665520/Teachers__Standards.pdf [Accessed 21 January 2019]

Didau, David (2019). The Learning Spy learning.spy.co.uk (online). Available from: https://learningspy.co.uk/ [Accessed 28 January 2019]

Dymoke, Sue (2012). *Reflective Teaching and Learning in the Secondary School*, 2nd Ed., London: Sage Publications, Ltd.

Education and Training Foundation (2014). Professional Standards for FE Teachers (on-line). Available from: http://www.et-foundation.co.uk/supporting/support-practitioners/professional-standards/ [Accessed 21 January 2019]

Ghaye, Tony (2011). *Teaching and Learning through Reflective Practice: A Practical Guide for Positive Action.* London: Routledge.

Hattie, John (2019). Visible Learning. Sebastian Waack, Co-Founder of Edkimo (online). Available from: https://visible-learning.org/ [Accessed 24 January 2019]

Holden, Gary (2016). National Standards for school-based initial teacher training mentors. Crown Copyright (online). Available from: https://assets.publishing.service.gov.uk/government/uploads/system/uploads/attachment_data/file/536891/Mentor_standards_report_Final.pdf [Accessed 28 January 2019]

Kolb, David A (2015). *Experiential Learning: Experience as the Source of Learning and Development.* Upper Saddle River, NJ: Pearson Education.

McAteer, Mary (2013). *Action Research in Education.* London: Sage Publications, Ltd./BERA.

McKenzie, Jill and Knapton, Helena (Autumn 2016). "The secret of engaging and effective coursework lessons." *Teaching Business & Economics* 21: 3.

Pollard, Andrew (2019). *Reflective Teaching in Schools*, 5th ed. London: Bloomsbury Academic.

researchEd (2019). (online) Available from: https://researched.org.uk/ [Accessed 28 January 2019]

Swain, Jon (2017). *Designing Research in Education: Concepts and Methodologies.* London: Sage Publications, Ltd.

The Sutton Trust (2011). The Education Endowment Foundation (online). Available from: https://educationendowmentfoundation.org.uk/ [Accessed 24 January 2019]

Walliman, Nicholas (2019). *Your Research Project: A Step-by-Step Guide for the First Time Researcher*, 3rd ed. London: Sage Publications Ltd.

INDEX